S0-CAU-044

Gary Henley

The QUIET REVOLUTION

The Recovery of New Testament Christianity in Our Day

Creation House
Carol Stream, Illinois

LIBRARY OF CONGRESS CATALOGUE CARD NUMBER: 79−131442

Unless otherwise indicated, Old Testament quotations are from the American Standard Version of 1901 and New Testament quotations are from the New American Standard Bible, New Testament, by permission of the Lockman Foundation.

Printed in the United States of America

CONTENTS

To

Bill

AUTHOR'S PREFACE

My purpose in writing this book is to make a positive statement about the exciting spontaneity of the Christian life and the glorious harmony this kind of Christian life enjoys with the simplicity of New Testament church life. The purpose has not been to make any kind of negative statement about any other understanding of Christianity or any other form of church life. This book is not a comment or critique on what has been. It is about the potential of something which could be even better. As a result I have largely chosen to avoid referring to the existing institutional church, choosing rather to allow the reader to draw his own conclusions as to the contrast between the new wineskins and what he sees about him on every hand.

However, because of this omission and because of the sometimes rather vivid contrast which is inferred, some may feel that I have "written off" the people in the institutional church as having no value and as being unusable so far as God is concerned. This is most emphatically not so. I feel that the great majority of God's true children are today involved to some degree in one form or another of institutional church life. So long as they are there, much good will doubtless be accomplished through these channels just as it has in the past. Most of us who are presently Christians have been converted as the result of the evangelistic efforts of other Christians who were part of the institutional church. It is also true that most of the great missionary endeavors have taken place within the framework of the institutional church. It is my conviction that God will always use any one of His people to the degree that that individual is available to Him. As someone has said, "God reserves the right to bless those who disagree with me!"

But let us not allow what has been accomplished in the past to prevent us from being objective and from asking ourselves a couple of pertinent questions. Do the spiritual accomplishments of the past really indicate God's stamp of approval on the various institutional forms which the church has taken, or only that God has used and blessed His people wherever He has found them, perhaps even at times in spite of incorrect doctrines or church forms rather than because of them? And can we dare assume that just because there have been some accomplishments that we have "arrived" at the point where we are all our Lord would have us to be as a church?

I have a deep conviction that the Lord is working mightily in these days to continue the preparation of His bride, the church, for His return. Few would deny that much has been regained since the Dark Ages. And now, in these critical days. God seems to be leading us on into more and more. Since the Reformation, God has repeatedly breathed out to His people truths lost and buried centuries before, as well as new and fresh supplies of His own life in successive waves of revival and renewal. But this time, instead of a revival or a renewal, the Spirit of the living God seems to be causing a *quiet revolution.*

There are three factors which cause me to identify the present work of the Lord in His church as a revolution. One of these is that a revolution is a type of warfare, and in these last and tumultous days we are experiencing spiritual warfare pitched to a far greater intensity than most of us have ever seen. But a revolution is not just ordinary warfare. It is warfare which is waged by the non-professional, non-uniformed citizen who is in the battle, not because of money or because he has been drafted, but because his heart has been deeply and profoundly affected. Again, this is what we are seeing and experiencing in the spiritual realm. This is a move of God's ordinary people — workingmen, housewives, young people — without theological training or other special qualifications, yet all suddenly becoming very active instruments in the hand of the Lord because of something He has done to turn their hearts and lives upside down.

And this brings us to the third and major reason that I refer to this movement as a revolution. There has never been a successful revolution which has not brought about great change. In this present spiritual revolution, as God's people become involved in spiritual warfare and victory, we also see them adjusting their manner of life and fellowship together in the direction of something which has a very familiar ring to anyone who has read the books of Acts recently.

In past years, the church has largely avoided the matter of change wherever it could. But more recently, the Word has been heard again and again. From the Vatican to the store-front missions, men are looking at the various forms of the institutional church and sensing the great need for change. And the change is inevitably coming. The question is, What will serve as the guide for change? Shall we consult the concepts and computors of finite man to build a church which will better suit God's purpose? Or shall we open the pages of God's Word, which always takes us back to the purity and simplicity of that which God breathed out to His apostles nearly two thousand years ago?

The *Quiet Revolution* is the move of the Spirit of God in our day to bring the people of God back to that spontaneous simplicity. It's quiet in the sense that there are no angry crowds, no effigies being burned, no signs of protest in the streets, no one angry at all as a matter of fact — just people filled with the joy of the presence of the Lord, learning to listen to and live by that which He has placed within. But it's a true revolution, nevertheless, and the eventual impact on the world may be greater than all the military, political, cultural, and economic revolutions which have ever taken place.

Part of this book deals with the various aspects of the life of the Spirit as God desires to see it lived out in the believer. The other part deals with what some would call the "form" of the church life of such Spirit-filled believers. The author is quick to acknowledge that spiritual life cannot be produced simply by adopting a form, whether that form is scriptural or not. But on the other hand, when God pours out His Spirit freely on His servants and handmaidens as He is today, there is need for concern as to what kind of wineskin will best contain and preserve the freshness and vitality of this new spiritual wine. The Quiet Revolution is neither a restoration of church form or a simple revival outpouring of God's Spirit alone. It is a move of the Spirit of God among His people to bring them into all the fulness which He has intended for them as His beloved church and bride.

But wherever there is change, there is also the new and the unknown and following that, fear and distrust. If ever there was a time when we need to keep our hearts open to one another and to love one another with the love of Jesus, it is now. As you read and as I write, my prayer is that you may "know the love of Christ which surpasses knowledge, that you may be filled up to all the fulness of God. Now to Him who is able to do exceeding abundantly beyond all that we ask or think, according to the power that works within us, to Him be the glory in the church and in Christ Jesus to all generations forever and ever. Amen."

1

TUNED IN, TURNED ON, AND – WATCH OUT!

Not long ago, in a gathering of a dozen young married couples, I had been sharing some of the things in this book. Afterward one of the men, a schoolteacher, came up to me and said, "You know, I really love God and I want to serve Him. I'm loyal to my church, but it just seems like nothing ever happens. I can't go on like this. I'm going to ask God to really show me where the action is." I thought, *Better fasten your seat belt, friend. If you really mean that, you're going to be covering some exciting ground in the days ahead.*

Someone once said, "If something doesn't happen pretty quick, something's going to happen." Apparently, he was right. Today, something is happening!

That "something" is a surging movement of twentieth-century Christians who are gathering together in small groups for a vital and intimate kind of fellowship which has been largely missing since the church of the New Testament. Like a nearly dormant two-thousand-year-old volcano, this movement has rumbled slightly now and then down through the ages. A few years ago, the surface was shaken a little more as the phenomenon began to gather momentum. Books began to be written. Conferences were held. Scholars theorized about the "role of the layman" in the church. But while they talked, others were gathering to share this newfound life with one another. The eruption had begun!

No, these Christians can't always tell you why they want to get together this way. And if they do, chances are the explanation will vary widely. But more and more the groups spring up. There are housewives and hippies, priests and Pentecostals, students, businessmen, young couples, and people of every description from every walk of life. They meet in homes, offices, church buildings, and out-of-doors. Some study the Bible, some pray, some share, some speak in tongues, some sing, and some do all of these and more. Some groups are related to large organizations and are part of a chain of dozens of identical groups with the same name. Other groups meet, never suspecting that another fellowship like their own exists. But nearly all would say that they have found something in this kind of fellowship which they had never had before, something they will never willingly be without again.

How did it all begin? Nobody really knows. The modern-day charismatic movement is responsible for much of it. Thousands have found new power and vitality, as well as spiritual gifts, in this encounter with the Spirit of God.

Many discovered that these things could not be expressed in the traditional churches where they had been attending, so they began to meet in homes to share with each other what God was doing in their lives. The writings of such men as Watchman Nee, Keith Miller, and Elton Trueblood have stirred many others to a realization that they need more than the usual Sunday morning service; that Christianity can be an exciting "company of the committed" who experience Christ on a daily basis.

On the college campus, groups like the Navigators, Campus Crusade for Christ, and Inter-Varsity have gathered students into small groups where they soon got a taste of something that was destined to quickly outgrow the vision of the very organizations which had spawned them. Then too, personal evangelism received new vigor through the stimulation provided by groups such as these. Many of the new converts came from a generation that looks with a critical objectivity at life and tends to reject that which is irrelevant and unworkable in their own lives. Many of these could not be interested in "going to church," but they would gather night after night to learn and share with one another.

Another category is made up of countless believers who are really trying to do a work for God: laymen, pastors, missionaries, and Christian workers on the front lines who were increasingly frustrated with small results, floundering converts, immature and apathetic fellow believers. Many of these began to have an increasing sense of the credibility gap between New Testament church experience and contemporary efforts. In desperation, they have turned to God and to the Scriptures with a new objectivity to find out what God really wants. Many have reached the conclusion that God breathed out to the early apostles a pattern of church life and fellowship which is the best possible container for the vitality and power of Spirit-filled Christians, and the ideal instrument for accomplishing the purpose of God in this world.

Basically, all these we have mentioned, and countless more, fit into one of two categories. There are the new believers who simply do not fit into institutional Christianity. And there are those rare birds, the seeking saints (Christians from both clergy and laity to whom God has begun to show something of the biblical teaching of true church life). Both categories share one thing in common: they have received "new wine" and they have discovered that it cannot be contained in old wineskins without being spilled and lost. Jesus made it plain: New wine must be placed in new wineskins. And today thousands of Christians who are tasting the new wine of the Spirit are discovering that the life it brings is an active, bubbling, ever expanding spiritual vitality which can only be contained by fresh and flexible wineskins. Most have tried to express this new life within the old traditional forms and have experienced the danger not only of spoiling the new wine but also of splitting and ruining the old wineskins. But there is good news. Many are discovering that God has made provision for *new wineskins,* designed nearly two thousand years ago, but appearing fresh today from the hand of God to hold the new wine of the twentieth century. The result is a kind of *revolution* as thousands of Christians who have experienced the new wine of the Spirit are also adjusting their lives and fellowships to the pattern God gave to the early disciples.

If you fit into one of these categories, this book was written for you. Where do I come in? Well, most of the descriptions in this chapter have applied to me at one time or another. Some still do. Converted in my twenties while working as a disc jockey, I floundered for several years in spiritual immaturity. It wasn't entirely because I wanted to. I didn't know where to begin. I remember knocking on a pastor's door early in my Christian life and asking, "What am I supposed to do?" I was given two books: one volume out of a very poor set of commentaries on the Bible and a book on door-to-door visitation written by someone who apparently had never done it. Later I was made an usher and finally promoted to director of the young people—a job I suspect they felt I qualified for because of my entertainment background. But all the time, I felt that there was something really big inside of me that somehow just wasn't coming out.

I didn't realize that these same feelings had been experienced at one time or another by most other Christians. I had no way of knowing that this was simply the new life that I had received trying to express itself, that the Holy Spirit within was trying to use me to bless others and reveal something of God to them in the regular course of everyday living. Instead, as the feeling grew stronger and the frustration increased, I began to interpret it as a call to the ministry. This all seemed very reasonable, especially since my church experience in those early days taught me that the clergyman seemed to be the only one who really had an adequate outlet for the kind of spiritual drives I was experiencing. So I soon left the broadcasting business to become a pastor in my denomination. At the time it seemed the only way. Perhaps for me, at that time and in that place, it was the only way God could have used to lead me another step down the road. As a pastor, I doubt that I was able to give much more help and direction to others than I had been given as a layman looking for answers. But it was while I was pastoring that I began to see the first threads of the pattern God was slowly to reveal. I began to see that the individual Christian is really important and that he ought to have something to share, a ministry, with both believers and unbelievers. I began to understand that the church would have to do a lot of changing if that were to become a reality. But I don't think I really believed that it could happen. I had tried to change the order of the communion service one Sunday morning and upset the whole congregation. How could we ever hope to make any serious adjustments? I decided that God would have to send persecution or something first, and until then I would have to wait.

Then came another open door: an opportunity to work with small groups of businessmen interdenominationally and to try to train laymen in personal evangelism. I thought if we couldn't change the church, maybe we could work with the same people alongside the institution as an arm of the church. I learned some wonderful things in those days, but there were still some of the same problems. It seemed that most of the men I worked with also had a local church and that this was their real spiritual priority. As long as we didn't say or do anything that contradicted their home church, all went well. But most seemed unable to grow beyond the limitations imposed by the churches they attended on Sunday. Meanwhile, for me, strategy conferences, fund-raising efforts, training institutes, evangelism campaigns, came and went, but the restlessness continued.

Most of this time I was never really happy with my own Christian life. I don't mean that I was chasing women or robbing banks, or even that I didn't feel led by the Spirit at times and see some spiritual results in the work. But under real pressure I didn't always act like Christ, and there were a good many people I couldn't really love—I just put up with them. Out of desperation, I went to God again and again. Who am I? What am I for? How can I please You?

In my desperation the answers began to come. God began to show my wife and me some of the basic secrets of Christian living we had never seen. Gradually, we began to experience a delightful kind of spontaneous Christianity as we simply learned to let Christ express Himself through us in daily living. At the same time, we became more and more certain that God wanted us to become part of a fellowship of Christians which found its life in the Spirit and its pattern in the Scriptures. Sporadically at first, and then more consistently, God began to bring a group of us together. We began to learn together the things which had only been theory in the past. We are still learning. Learning to be honest, learning to be committed to one another, learning to love. And learning more all the time about the church that God wants to see. The resulting fellowship is not by any means an accurate expression of a New Testament church but it is as close as anything I have ever personally seen or experienced. Better yet, it is an atmosphere where each one can be open and honest and where each one has an opportunity to share what he or she has without fear of rejection.

This may be where you are. Or maybe you are one of those who have never even thought about these things before and this book is your first exposure. Perhaps you are part of some little group which has been meeting for a while with only limited success. Or you might be miles ahead of the rest of us. If you are the latter, love us. If you are anything else, this book may help you.

Out of the thousands of groups of Christians who are meeting for regular fellowship, only a small percentage seem to realize what they really are. Many only know that it has been a great stimulus to their growth in Christ and have no idea that what they are doing may be actually more biblical than the vast majority of institutional churches about them. Many don't even recognize what they are doing as "church," but as something supplemental. Without a good scriptural understanding of the church, these groups are highly vulnerable to attacks of Satan and to a real limitation of life as they move along.

On the other hand, there are groups of believers who have caught something of the pattern of the New Testament church and are trying to reproduce it mechanically. This can be death. For these there is a great need to see the spontaneity of the fellowship of the body of Christ. There is a pattern in the Scriptures, but it is the result not the cause of spiritual life.

But in spite of these problems, God is drawing people from all of these backgrounds to a common experience with Christ and with one another in the body of Christ. The years to come will see a great restoration of the precepts, power, and pattern of New Testament church life. Like the successive waves of an incoming tide, each genuine move of God since the Reformation has risen a little higher than those preceding it, recovering ground which was lost by the ebbing tide of a backsliding church in the earlier centuries of Christianity. God's goal is to recover the entire beach, to prepare a church for His return which is like the church He left behind. He is pouring out His Spirit upon all flesh and the Spirit of truth is beginning to teach His people about the new wineskins which are so much a part of God's plan for those who receive His new wine.

The strength of New Testament fellowship is this new wine in the lives of individual believers who have learned to live the spontaneous Christ-life. For this reason I want to begin by sharing what I have discovered about what God wants to do in and through us as individual Christians. From there we'll go on to the new wineskins, to what God wants to do in and through His church, the body of Christ. But first we will need a good grasp on the foundation of what we are and of

His purpose for our lives. That foundation was laid in the creation of the world, for God's purpose has not changed. Let's look together at what God had in mind for our mutual granddaddy, Adam. We'll see that it has a direct bearing on how to live victoriously day by day and to enjoy the fulfilling experience of fellowship with God's people today.

2

WHO, WHERE, WHEN, AND *WHY?*

That which is known about God is evident within them; for God made it evident to them. For since the creation of the world His invisible attributes, His eternal power and divine nature, have been clearly seen, being understood through what has been made (Romans 1:19-20).

Did you ever ask yourself, What is it really all about? I have, both before and after I became a Christian. I can remember that even as a kid in Idaho I used to have a sort of mysterious sense of destiny. It was as though I existed for some special reason, but it was never very apparent what that reason was. After I came to Christ, I learned that I was "saved to serve." That helped, but there were still a lot of unanswered questions. Like, What is God's purpose? I was told it was to save sinners from hell. Well, then, why would He create the world in the first place? He must have known we were going to foul it up, and He could have saved Himself the effort. More than that, He could have saved His Son by not creating any people to sin in the first place. No, I really couldn't buy that. There had to be more to it. I kept asking, but it seemed that none of the answers I got were big enough to fit God. To be honest, there have been times when I wondered if Christianity really makes any sense at all. Then, slowly, I began to discover that I had been selling the Bible short by accepting these superficial explanations. The truth is there! God has a purpose for this world—a purpose for you and for me that is as big as Himself! And He had that purpose in mind before He even started to create.

"In the beginning God" (Genesis 1:1). It used to be that just about the only value those words had for me was to serve as fuel for an argument against evolution. Now, they tell me something exciting about myself, something about *why* I am. Because that's when I began: in the mind of God at a time when only God existed.

Hard to grasp, isn't it? Nothing but God. No other life, thought, energy, matter, form, or being existed. In fact, there wasn't even an idea for anything else apart from God's idea. Only God existed—the original, uncreated life of God. When the Bible uses the term *eternal life,* it is this life of God that it refers to. His is the only life which is eternal. Everything else began when, "In the beginning God created . . . ."

But why did He create? Surely He was complete in Himself. Well, it is true that He didn't need anything. But the very nature of God almost demands worship. All through the Bible the cry of the Spirit-led man is praise to God. "All thy works shall give thanks unto thee, O Jehovah; and thy saints shall bless thee" (Psalm 145:10). God Himself decreed that this will be: "As I live, says the Lord, every knee shall bow to Me, and every tongue shall give praise to God" (Romans 14:11).

But there is a problem. How can God be worshiped unless He is known? And how can God, who is spirit, be known in a physical, tangible universe? God solved the problem by placing within His creation various things which would reveal something about Himself. And what God wants today, more than anything else, is something through which He can express His nature so that it can be seen and appreciated by His universe. That something is the church of Jesus Christ, a body in which God is expressed. The church is God's primary means of revealing Himself to our generation. But, in the beginning, God created a number of things which were intended to tell us something of Himself.

One example is light. God created light. But the created

light we see in the sun or electric bulb is only a created copy of some aspect of God. For the Bible says that Jesus is "the light of the world" (John 8:12) and that His "life was the light of men" (John 1:4). Someday, we'll live in a city whose only light will be God (Revelation 21:23). But for now, the created light can help us to know something about God.

So it is with many other created things. The trees tell us that it is the nature of God's life to produce fruit after its kind. The wind expresses something about the Holy Spirit. So does the dove. The lowly lamb is used many times to help us understand the Lord's sacrifice for us on the cross. Psalm 148 points out that virtually every aspect of creation expresses something of God and brings praise to His name.

But in that psalm, as in the story of creation, the climax of those things created to express God is man. God chose man to be the highest expression of the nature of God which could be seen in this present world. "To the end that we. . . should be to the praise of His glory" (Ephesians 1:12). This is what you and I are really all about.

What is so special about man? Is he really more than a high-grade animal? Why does he keep inventing religions and talking about having a higher destiny? Why does he persist with this idea that he is something other than a creature of this world alone, with a life that somehow goes on after death? This is an idea which has never even occurred to any other form of animal life. Why? What is so different about man? I discovered that God created you and me to express Himself more perfectly than could anything else in the universe. If we are to know how we fit into God's long-range goal, we need to understand just how He has uniquely prepared and equipped us for the job. If we are going to please Him, as individuals and as the church, we need to know what we are as He created us.

And God said, Let us make man in our image, after our likeness: and let them have dominion over the fish of the sea, and over the birds of the heavens, and over the cattle, and over all the earth, and over every creeping thing that creepeth upon the earth. And God created man in his own image, in the image of God created he him; male and female created he them (Genesis 1:26-27).

And Jehovah God formed man of the dust of the ground, and breathed into his nostrils the breath of life; and man became a living soul (Genesis 2:7).

These descriptions are brief but important. Our creation was no simple "let there be light" matter. For while many created things were to express God in some way, only man is chosen to be conformed to His image.

The first thing God did was to form the dust of the earth into a body. Our purpose of expressing God in a physical world requires a body. We'll talk more about that body later, but for now I want to mention that as God created it there was nothing evil about the body of man. It was good and wonderfully suited in every way to serve God's purpose.

But a body alone is not enough. It had been just a hunk of clay lying on the ground. God went into action. He "breathed into his nostrils the breath of life; and man became a living soul." Now man has life. But it is really important at this point to see that the life this man has is not divine life as yet. God made him live by breathing on him, and many people assume that this is when God gave man the Holy Spirit. I don't think so. While it was the Spirit of God doing the work, the life He gave to man was only human, or soul-type, life at this point.

Look at what happened: "Man became *a living soul.*" The word which is translated "living soul" is translated "life" in Genesis 1:30 and "creature" in Genesis 1:24. There it refers to the life that God gave to the birds and animals. In short, God gave to both man and animals a quality of life which is described as a "living soul." Now there is no question but that man received a higher form of this conscious life than the other creatures. But it was still only soul-life, and soul-life in itself is not capable of causing man to be an expression of God. This requires divine life, the life of the Spirit of God. At this point, man had only become a living soul. Receiving the life of God was to be another step for him.

Paul points up the difference in this verse: "The first man, Adam, became a living soul. The last Adam [Christ] became a life-giving spirit" (1 Corinthians 15:45).

The day I first really saw this, it hit me like a ton of bricks. I was in a conference in Kansas City with a dozen or so other Christian workers who had begun to see that something was amiss in the organized church. We had come together to talk about how to get it straightened out. We were serious and we were doing something about it. At the time I was working on a campaign in which we had formed over 700 home Bible studies and trained 1,200 people in personal evangelism. We were using every modern form of communication and promotion we knew to do the work of the Lord. Then came the conference. A man spoke to us for two hours the first evening and completely destroyed the foundations of everything that I was doing. It was especially devastating because the man was Gene Edwards, the fellow who had first taught me to do personal evangelism five years earlier. At that time he had been traveling around the country doing the same kind of thing I was now doing. Then suddenly he dropped out of sight for five years until he showed up at that conference. Where had he been? Someplace where he had been learning by experience what God had sent him back into my life that night to show to me.

The simple truth he shared that night was the difference between the human soul-life that man received at creation and the divine life of the Spirit which we can also have. I had had both for years, but I had never clearly distinguished between the two. The result was that I was doing a great deal of the Lord's work in the strength of my human life while under the impression that it was all of the Spirit. This distinction may not seem important to you right now, but I have found it to be one of the most important keys to successful Christian living and ministry. The Bible says that the Word of God is able to help you make this distinction clearly (Hebrews 4:12) and I trust this is going to happen as we move along.

So far, we see man as a lump of clay, activated by the addition of human life. But God's purpose is so much more! We are to be like Him, "to be conformed to the image of His Son" (Romans 8:29). How can this be?

In the New Testament, Paul describes God as a potter who, when He shaped man of clay, shaped him as a vessel, a clay pot designed to contain something (Romans 9:20-21). Not just a lump, but a vessel with an interior, suited for a purpose beyond its own existence alone. And Paul adds:

> *He did so in order that He might make known the riches of His glory upon vessels of mercy, which He prepared beforehand for glory, even us (Romans 9:23-24).*

You and I are vessels of mercy, chosen by God and specifically designed as containers for something. And our purpose is to make known the riches of His glory.

Second Corinthians 4:6 tells us that the glory of God is vested in Jesus. Verse 7 says:

> *We have this treasure in earthen vessels, that the surpassing greatness of the power may be of God and not from ourselves.*

And this is what man is all about! A clay pot—man's body with its human life, designed to contain a treasure, the glory of God in Jesus Christ. And the reason for this peculiar combination is that no one will ever think that the radiance of the treasure is a result of the clay pot in which it has been placed. There is a great lesson for us here: Nothing which has its origin in man's human soul-life alone is useful in fulfilling God's ultimate purpose of bringing glory to Himself.

Paul goes on: ". . .that the life of Jesus also may be manifested in our body" and, ". . .that the life of Jesus also may be manifested in our mortal flesh" (2 Corinthians 4:10-11). While the container is human and mortal, yet the life which must be expressed must be His own if God is to be glorified.

In Chicago, I knew a sixteen-year-old girl who had been rather recently added to the Lord. A sullen, alienated girl, she had had several brushes with the law and had spent weeks sitting in her room, smoking pot and trying to write a book about Robert Kennedy before she came to know Christ. But not long afterward, her woman parole officer suddenly asked one day, "Cindy, what's happened to you? You have changed more in the last few weeks than any other girl I have ever worked with. You actually act like you love me. What's gotten into you?" The parole officer was closer than she thought. "Something" had "gotten into" Cindy. And that something was obviously more than the human life of the clay container.

I think you can see that Adam was innocent as God created him, but that he still had a way to go before he could really fulfill God's purpose for him. His little clay body, with its human soul-life, just wasn't able in itself to express the nature of God. God is love, and He wants the world to know it. So He made man with a container which could contain the very life of God itself. This is what makes man different. Body and soul are just not enough. There must be more!

3

THERE MUST BE MORE!

And Jehovah God formed man of the dust of the ground (Genesis 2:7).

Jehovah. . .formeth the spirit of man within him (Zechariah 12:1).

For the word of God is living and active and sharper than any two-edged sword, and piercing as far as the vision of soul and spirit (Hebrews 4:12).

So far, we know that God created man to express God's life and nature in this world so that God can be known and praised. In order to achieve this, God made man in a very special way. He gave man something He didn't give to the animals, a container for the life of God "that the life of Jesus. . . may be manifested in our body" (2 Corinthians 4:10).

The apostle Paul explains what this container is. He says that man is not just soul and body, but spirit, soul, and body (1 Thessalonians 5:23). When God formed the clay, He made a vessel with an interior "space" to be filled with His own life. That "space" is the human spirit. You and I are higher than the animals but lower than the angels. We are the bridge between God and the world, so we are both physical and spiritual. Like the animals, we have a body with a life of its own, but like God, who is a Spirit, we also have a spirit. Our human spirit is the container for the uncreated eternal life of God. Pascal, the great mathematician and philosopher, said, "There is a God-shaped vacuum in the heart of each man which cannot be satisfied by any created thing, but only by God the creator, made known through Jesus Christ."

A very important key to the Christian life is the ability to tell the difference between the spirit and the soul. The spirit has a number of functions which are far beyond the soul. One of the reasons the present-day church so often fails to fulfill the purpose of God is the great amount of soulish activity which is carried out in the name of the "work of the Lord." I knew one pastor who offered free helicopter rides as a prize for bringing the most visitors to Sunday school. That's a rather extreme example of soulishness in Christian work, of course, but it points up our great need to see clearly the differences between spirit, soul, and body, as well as to see how all three can work together to allow the life of Jesus to be expressed.

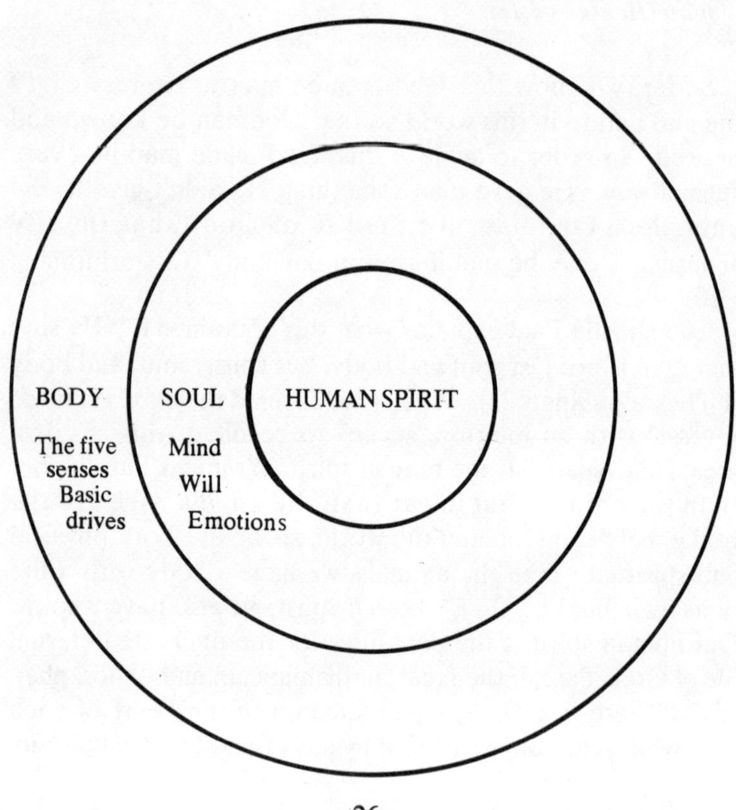

THE BODY

Your body is flesh, blood, and bone, but that's not all. Because the body is the outermost part of man, God has equipped it with the five senses so that you can respond to your environment. As I first began to see the Spirit really controlling my own life, I was amazed at how lonely people began to sound. In every conversation it seemed they just poured out their troubles. Was this something new? Or had I just been walking in the flesh so much that my ears had not been available to my spirit? As I learned to make my ears available to Jesus, it seemed that I was kept busy using them to love people by just listening to the troubles no one else had time for. When the senses are controlled by the Spirit of God, they allow you to be aware of your surroundings so that you can respond to life about you with the love of God. But on the other hand, when the body with its five senses operates independently from God's control, they become the open gate through which the world gains entrance to a man and draws him away from God's purpose. (See James 1:14.)

Your body also has basic drives which influence your behavior. These are essentially hunger, survival and sex. They were also given by God for a purpose, and make a positive contribution as long as they are in submission to the spirit. Uncontrolled, of course, they do become the source of untold agony, cruelty, and evil in this cursed world. Many Christians seem to be afraid of their bodies, thinking that they are something which is always anti-God. This is not true. It's just that the body was not made to be self-controlling, that's all. We need to see the role of the spirit. For instance, I know of several marriages which have greatly improved since the man and wife began to see the beautiful Spirit-led balance and harmony brought into marriage by the sex drive when it is directed by the Lord.

Really, the body is just a dwelling place, an "earthly house" (2 Corinthians 5:1-2) which we have in common with all forms of created life, both animal and vegetable. All of these grow, reproduce, and react to the surroundings. But there is a higher kind of behavior which belongs to the animal kingdom and has its seat in the soul.

THE SOUL

The soul of man is that intelligent, willful life which he shares with other animals to some degree. Of course, he is not only an animal, but we need to realize that a great part of his being is this soulish-animal life.

The soul of man has three parts: mind, will and emotion. In the natural man the soul receives almost everything through the five senses of the body and in turn controls the body in its reactions toward the outside world.

The Bible teaches that part of the soul of man is his mind, or intelligence. It says the soul "knows" things (Proverbs 19:2), needs knowledge (Psalm 13:2), considers various courses of action (Psalm 139:14), and remembers (Lamentations 3:20).

It's interesting that in some verses, the Hebrew word for soul is actually translated "will." "Deliver me not over unto the *will* of mine adversaries" (Psalm 27:12). This and other verses tell us that one function of the soul of man is choice through the will. If this God-given will is turned toward God, it will result in man coming into the purpose for which he was created.

We have also been equipped by God with a rich variety of emotions. The Bible declares that the human capacity to love, hate, pity, grieve, worry, be discouraged, and experience many other aspects of emotion all spring from the human soul. A rich emotional capacity is something to be thankful for, but it does need the control of the Spirit or it can lead man into a great deal of trouble.

We come in contact with and become aware of the outside world through the body. But the soul is within and helps us to become aware of our self. The Bible sometimes calls man's soul the "self" (see Luke 9:23-25). You might call the soul the personality of man. It is here that he comes to know himself. Later we will see that it is in his spirit he comes to know God.

It's obvious that man needs only body and soul to live like an animal, to survive and reproduce. But he often doesn't realize that this is what he's doing. Without God, he goes along spiritually empty, yet carving out a life for himself which almost convinces him that he needs nothing else. Spiritually dead, he is very much soulishly alive. This is where I had a very big problem and still do sometimes. You see, I had been living by my own mind, will, and emotion for so long before I became a Christian that I didn't know anything else. My soul was "over-developed" and when I became a new Christian it just went right on controlling things. Not that my life looked the same, of course. In my mind I knew I was supposed to be different. My emotions told me I wanted to please God and my Christian friends. So I just brought my willpower into play and began to act differently. Since no one taught me that this was wrong, I assumed it was right and that growing in the Christian life was a matter of knowing more, wanting it more, and trying harder. Gary Henley was still in control and Gary Henley was getting mighty tired and frustrated. All because I didn't know my soul from my spirit. Read the fourth chapter of the book of Hebrews and you'll find that the reason many believers never enter into the "rest of God" is this very problem.

Before we leave the soul and go on to the spirit, I want to mention that while man's human life is very much like the animal soul, there are at least two ways in which they differ. One is the capacity for moral responsibility, and the other is the destiny of his soul after physical death.

By moral responsibility, I mean a response to truth.

It is interesting to note, that only man within the animal kingdom is capable of producing words and recognizing them to any great extent in order to convey and receive exact items of information: to hear, utter—or to distort—the Truth. Maybe his capacity for speech plays a far bigger part than we had thought in man's capacity to behave as a moral being. It lays him open to the word.[1]

In this way, even in his soul-life, man rises above the animals in his ability to know and be held accountable for truth. "For by your words you shall be justified, and by your words you shall be condemned" (Matthew 12:37).

Secondly, man was created not just for this world but to go on singing the praises of God forever. God has provided for this by bringing man's soul into contact with his spirit, giving the soul the ability to survive after death.

As the marrow within the joints, so is the human spirit buried deep within the human soul, remaining essentially distinct, yet together forming that complete immaterial entity capable of endless survival after physical death, as opposed to the purely "animal soul" common to the rest of the animal kingdom, which possesses no such capacity either to survive or to be held morally responsible beyond the grave.[2]

Both of these were involved when I first came to know Christ. I claimed to be an atheist. One night while working in a radio station, I was suddenly confronted with the news that a man I knew, another disc jockey, had drowned. Immediately the thought struck me that someday I was going to die—then what? Here was something that I couldn't handle in my own boastful self-sufficiency. Then parts of various verses of Scripture that I had heard began flashing through my mind. I can't even tell you now what they were—some verses that mentioned God and some that talked about life after death and about judgment. But in that flash of a second I recognized truth: God does exist and someday I am going to face Him. Even though I didn't know what to do about it at that moment, I couldn't get away from those two simple truths. They haunted me for several days until I finally turned to Christ. I *was* different than an animal, even though I had denied it, and God had used that difference to bring me to Himself.

THE HUMAN SPIRIT

The spirit of man is the noblest and most essential part of his being if he is to be truly a man and not just an animal. When Genesis 1:27 says that God created man to be "in his image," obviously it is not talking about His physical form, for God doesn't have a physical form. We don't even know what God looks like, for "no man has seen God at any time" (John 1:18). Then how can we have His image?

Jesus said, "God is spirit" (John 4:24). God created our bodies from dust and man became a living soul. But Zechariah tells us that when God shaped this clay pot, He "formeth the spirit of man within him" (Zechariah 12:1). And so man became higher than the animals in yet another way: he became a spiritual creature equipped to live on a spiritual plane for a spiritual purpose. It is the spirit of man which makes possible all the spiritual functions which make him a complete man.

The primary function of the human spirit is containing God. God's contact with man is in the spirit (2 Timothy 4:22) and it is through the spirit that He makes His influence upon the soul and body.

Jesus said, "I am in My Father, and you in Me, and I in you" (John 14:20). Jesus was speaking of an inner, spiritual relationship which He had with the Father. We are intended to enter into the same relationship with Jesus. This relationship is a merger, or blending, of God's Spirit with man's spirit, so that it can be equally said that He is in me or that I am in Him. "The one who joins himself to the Lord is one spirit with Him" (1 Corinthians 6:17). It's something like pouring a cup of ink and a cup of water together in a bowl. Would you say the ink is in the water or the water is in the ink? Both statements are true, but really the two liquids have become one. Sometimes scholars have difficulty translating verses in the Bible which refer to the spirit. One translation will have the word *spirit* capitalized, while another puts it in lowercase letters. (E.g., compare Romans 8:10 in the King James Version and New American Standard Bible.) It's difficult to decide in some of these verses whether God, the Holy Spirit or man's spirit is referred to, because the identification is so complete. Praise God, we are one with Him!

"Do you not know that you are a temple of God, and that the Spirit of God dwells in you?" (1 Corinthians 3:16). The temple of God in the Old Testament had three parts: the outer court; the holy place; and deep within, the holiest of all, the most holy place, where the glory of God dwelt. So it is today with man, the temple of God: the body; the soul; and the most holy place of the spirit, where man meets with God to know, serve, and worship Him.

Knowing God is another function of the human spirit. Spiritual things must be known by spirit.

> *The natural [lit., soul-type] man does not accept the things of the Spirit of God; for they are foolishness to him, and he cannot understand them, because they are spiritually appraised [examined, understood]. But he who is spiritual appraises all things (1 Corinthians 2:14-15).*

The natural man is described as "soul-type" because he has lost his spirit function. His body and soul live, his mind is keen, but his spirit has died and his ability to grasp spiritual things is gone. You see, the human mind as a function of the soul is not able to know spiritual truth. It is able to absorb and systematize facts *about* spiritual things, but these things must be revealed and made alive in the spirit. The spirit uses the mind to help us understand, and even to allow us to explain to others, but the knowing is in the spirit.

I once learned a great lesson about this from a Christian named Harry. Harry had been a Christian for many years, a deacon in the organized church, and a Sunday school teacher. Then Harry had a fresh experience with the Spirit of God and his life was miraculously changed. Among other things God showed him was that the Holy Spirit is not only the Spirit of power but also the Spirit of truth! Harry began to practice 1 John 2:27, studying the Scriptures with a real expectation that the Lord would reveal in the Spirit just what He wanted Harry to see. When I met him he couldn't stop talking about the miracle that had resulted. He had learned more of God in a few months on his knees than he had in years with his mind and his commentaries.

Worshiping God also requires the spirit.

> *The true worshipers shall worship the Father in spirit and in truth; for such people the Father seeks to be His worshipers. God is spirit; and those who worship Him must worship in spirit and truth (John 4:23-24).*
>
> *We are the true circumcision, who worship in the Spirit of God and glory in Christ Jesus and put no confidence in the flesh (Philippians 3:3).*

Recently we had several college students from the South meet with us in our Sunday gathering. One of the young men was facing the draft, and he was really concerned about the direction the Lord would have him to take in this. We chatted about it for a little while, but before it got into a soulish tossing back and forth of human opinions we felt led to take it to the Lord in prayer. We prayed for a considerable period of time; then as the Holy Spirit began to gently minister to the young man on the matter, we moved into a real time of praise and thanksgiving to the Lord for loving us and being concerned about us in a personal way. There were no sermons; there was little singing; there was nothing that was preplanned as "worship." But after the meeting one of the college girls remarked that she had been in church all of her life and had never seen real worship until that day.

Worshiping in Spirit and in truth is simply letting the Spirit bring us together with God in the way that He desires for that time. It might never be done just the same again, for we have found that the Spirit is so original that He seldom repeats Himself. I have been in gatherings where the Spirit has led in worship not for twenty minutes or an hour but for hours without any sense of restlessness in the worshipers.

Serving God is a function of the spirit which is probably more frequently overlooked than any other. Paul wrote, "God whom I serve in my spirit. . ., is my witness" (Romans 1:9). If there is any area in which man is tempted to utilize all the resources of his human soul-life, it is in service for God.

We live in a world of soul-order. Man has so many well-developed attributes and ingenious inventions to drag over into the realm of spiritual work. He learns to "grow spiritually" through self-improvement methods borrowed from Dale Carnegie. He learns to witness by memorizing good sales techniques. He runs the church with the latest big-business organizational skills. And some of the chief "gifts" which stand out are administrative ability, a keen mind, sparkling personality, glib tongue, and professionally developed musical talent. Yet Paul writes:

My message and my preaching were not in persuasive words of wisdom, but in demonstration of the Spirit and of power, that your faith should not rest on the wisdom of men, but on the power of God (1 Corinthians 2:4-5).

What's wrong here? Simply that many of God's people don't discern between soul and spirit. They often work in the power of the soul while assuming they are in the Spirit. We need to know that:

The weapons of our warfare are not of the flesh, but divinely powerful (2 Corinthians 10:4).

For our struggle is not against flesh and blood, but against the rulers, against the powers, against the world-forces of this darkness, against the spiritual forces of wickedness in the heavenly places (Ephesians 6:12).

Witnessing is only one way of serving God, of course. For several years I majored in teaching Christians how to witness. More recently I have concentrated on sharing with new Christians what it means to live by the Spirit of life. Some of the most effective witnesses I know have never been told "how" to share Christ. But they regularly do it as a spontaneous expression of the life and love of God within them.

But this is hard to learn if your soul has some well-developed gifts of its own. A very good friend of mine was a skilled trumpet player in the navy band when he came to know Christ. Afterward, Christians encouraged him to "play his horn for the Lord." For five years he went from meeting to meeting triple-tonguing and slurring with his trumpet, using all the tricks of the trade to entertain the saints. Then God showed him that to really serve God the gift must come from the Spirit. The horn went into the case where it remains to this day, and in its place God has given a wonderful ministry of teaching, especially on a man-to-man basis with hungry individuals. Many of the things in this book were taught to me by this same man—the man without the horn.

This is not to say that there is no place for a ministry of music among God's people. To the contrary, some have been greatly used by God in this way. But it is important that we each seek God to learn what our ministries are and to use them only under the prompting and anointing of the Spirit. We should not assume that because we happen to have such-and-such a natural ability, this is our gift, or ministry. And it is especially important that we don't try to serve God with some ability in which we have such confidence that we feel we don't need to really depend upon the Spirit.

"The spirit of man is the lamp of Jehovah" (Proverbs 20:27). As a lamp, its purpose is to show forth a light. But John wrote, "The life was the light" (John 1:4). The lamp itself is not the light, and certainly the lampstand (body and soul) is not the light. What electricity is to a light bulb, what oil is to an oil lamp, the life of God is to the human spirit. God's desire is to fill you with the oil of the Holy Spirit, causing you to be spiritually alive, so that, in complete dependence upon that limitless supply of oil, you might manifest the light and life which is Jesus Christ in your mortal body!

The primary need among believers today is not simply to be saved and on the way to heaven, nor even to assist others to find Christ. It is to become men who live by the life of God in the spirit, so that man can again be truly man, and God can be known, worshiped, and served in spirit and in truth!

WHAT HAPPENED TO ADAM?

We saw that Adam had been created body and soul and had been given a human spirit so that he might contain the life of God. Only by this could he go beyond innocence to the perfection of God's purpose. His education was just trees. These seem to represent something more than ordinary trees, for one of them. the tree of life, exists eternally (cf. Revelation 22:2). It represents the eternal life of the Spirit of God. The other, the tree of knowledge of good and evil, had the purpose of serving as the test for Adam and Eve. But Satan, the spirit of Antichrist, used the good thing that God had placed there to lead them astray. This wicked spirit is still persuading men to develop their human lives so that they can live independently from the indwelling life of God.

All Adam had to do was to eat of the tree of life and he could have begun to live and grow spiritually into the image of God, perfectly fulfilling God's purpose for him. "Christ in you, the hope of glory" (Colossians 1:27). "So he who eats Me, he also shall live because of Me" (John 6:57).

But there was another possibility. He was not to eat of the other three. So there were two ways to go. What if he went the wrong way?

There lay the hidden lesson. Humans are containers, to be possessed by another spirit in the human spirit. They are slaves to be bossed. (Romans 6:16) They do not boss themselves. . . .

There was the tree of life, all the positive power in it to do the right and resist the wrong, for that tree was Christ. Adam never so much as glanced in its direction, because it never dawned on him that humans are basically helpless, and that his deliverance could not be in his own resistance, but only in the counter action of the Spirit of Truth within him, if he took of Him. He never did. . . .He remained a recipient, for man always is that, but he received the wrong spirit through the wrong tree—"the spirit that now worketh in the children of disobedience," the spirit of self-sufficiency, the spirit of self-love, the spirit of error.[3]

The result was devastating—it was death! Spiritual death is not annihilation but being cut off from life. It is not that there is no more human spirit in man, but that it is numb, as when a man is in a coma. Whatever capacity it had to know or serve God is paralyzed.

Satan tempted man by appealing to his soul-life and by arousing it to a rebellion over the spirit. Now the pattern is set. Cut off from spiritual life, man began to develop his soul until it has become so totally dominant that he forgets that he even has a spirit. Stronger and stronger the soul becomes until it seems that man can do almost anything—anything but what he is supposed to do: express the nature of God.

The death in his spirit spread through his soul to his body, and man became what we see today: a deadened, darkened spirit, a twisted, overdeveloped soul, and a decaying body. The Bible calls this fellow the "old man." The old man is not merely a minor part of the individual; it is all that we inherit from Adam, both morally and judicially. It is the corrupt human nature, the natural man.

Romans 6:6 tells us that the "old man" is a slave to sin. Now we can see why. Without a spirit alive to God, he is cut off from the provision of God's godliness. Everything he does is done independently of God, and independence from God is the essence of sin. Because he cannot act other than independently from God, he is a slave to sin.

Another term, *the flesh,* is important here. In many cases of its use in the New Testament, *flesh* does not refer to man's physical body. Nor does it refer to the old man, as many seem to think. It is easy to see how this confusion arises, however. *Flesh* refers to the principle of the body and soul acting independently from the spirit, whether in the believer or in the unbeliever (cf. Romans 8:4-8; Galatians 5:16-25). When the body and soul act to express the human life of man, the origin and control are not of the spirit, so they are of the flesh. In the old man there is no active spirit to control and direct him; therefore all that he does is in the flesh.

THE OLD MAN

Without God's Spirit in his human spirit, his human life (body and soul) always acts independently from God. Such independent actionin sin. Thus the old man (or natural man) is a slave to sin.

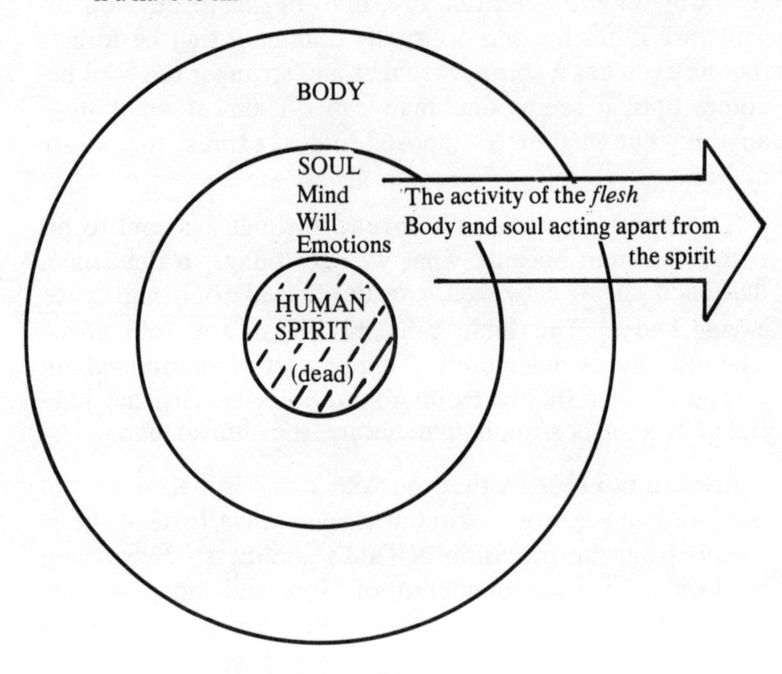

With the Christian, the "new man," it is another matter. He has a living spirit, and he is capable of allowing it to control his entire being. Of course, he also has a body and soul which can still act apart from his spirit if he desires them to, and thus he too can walk in the flesh. But he doesn't have to do this! The old man is dead, but the new man can act like the old man by simply ignoring the spirit and acting in the flesh. The important thing is that while the old man has no choice but to walk in the flesh and to sin, the new man at all times has the choice of obeying the spirit and expressing the righteousness of God (Romans 8:4; Galatians 5:16-25). The new man does not have to act in the flesh, and so sin is not his rightful master!

The potential of a man equipped with the wholeness of spirit, soul, and body is staggering. The problem is that we inherit a very different man from Adam. He lacks the basic ingredient, the life of God within his human spirit. For God's purpose to be fulfilled, this life must somehow be restored to him, and he must learn what he failed to learn in the garden: to take in that life continually and live by it. The way God has met this problem is the most exciting discovery I have ever made. The next chapter tells the *how* of the greatest mystery the world has ever known: *How* to be like Jesus!

4

HOW?

Great is the mystery of godliness: He who was revealed in the flesh (1 Timothy 3:16).

God's mystery, that is, Christ Himself (Colossians 2:2).

The glory of this mystery. . ., which is Christ in you, the hope of glory (Colossians 1:27).

Christ, who is our life. . . (Colossians 3:4).

God wants a tangible expression of His own life in this world. Somehow, men have always known in their hearts that they should be like God. But the question is, How? From the time that Adam sinned, until the cross of Calvary, it was a mystery. But rejoice! It's a mystery no more! You and I have been let in on the secret: *Christ is the mystery!*

> *What was from the beginning, what we have heard, what we have seen with our eyes, what we beheld and our hands handled, concerning the Word of Life—and the life was manifested, and we have seen and bear witness and proclaim to you the eternal life, which was with the Father and was manifested to us (1 John 1:1-2).*

Jesus was the perfect expression of the life of God. He was seen, touched, known, and heard, yet the life He expressed was not His own but the Father's. The exciting thing is that we're to live the same way. Jesus lived by the life of the Father in Him. Now we are to live by His life in us.

He said "I came that they might have life, and might have it abundantly" (John 10:10). What did He mean? Not just human life; mankind already had that. Nor was it a better fed and clothed human life; nor even the peace and assurance of a man who knows that he is forgiven and going to heaven.

Abundant life is not just an abundant *way* of life. It is an abundant supply of that which really *is* life! Not just more of the synthetic imitation we already have, but the actual indwelling of that life from which all the others were copied. What is abundant life? It is the actual presence of Jesus Christ, filling our spirit and flooding our entire being. It is nothing less than His life, and it is abundant because it was for the purpose of containing that life that we were created. He came to give us Himself!

THE NEW MAN

"And. . .you were dead in your trespasses and sins. . . .But God. . .made us *alive* together. . .with Christ" (Ephesians 2:1-5, Amplified Bible).

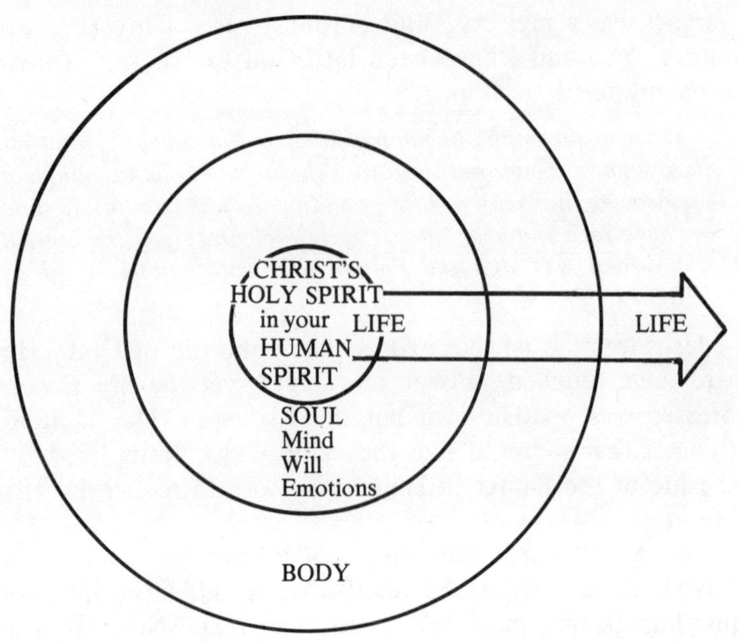

Many people think of eternal life as the time they will spend in heaven. Eternal life is not a time, and it is not a thing. Eternal life dwells in God. When we have eternal life, we have God in the person of His Son, Jesus Christ. God now dwells in my body, and that affects far more than the future. It affects the present!

> *And you [He made alive], when you were dead [slain] by [your] trespasses and sins. . . .He made us alive together in fellowship and in union with Christ. He gave us the very life of Christ Himself, the same new life with which He quickened Him (Ephesians 2:1-5, Amplified Bible).*

This, then, is Christianity! Jesus Christ has come to live in you! And this is the mystery of godliness—His life in you is an active force which will simply behave like He is: godly.

The first time I was aware of this happening in my Christian life I didn't even know what it was. I had always had a terrific temper which would break out when some-one crossed me. One day, not long after I became a Christian, I was driving with my wife in a brand-new car we had just bought. Suddenly another car shot out from a side street and hit my front fender, causing considerable damage. I got out of the car, exchanged the necessary in-formation with the other driver, smiled, and got back into the car. It was then that my wife asked me if I realized that I hadn't blown up. I hadn't even thought about it. My behavior was just a spontaneous expression of the life of Jesus. The problem, of course, was that because I didn't know what was happening, I wasn't consistent after that. One time I would be an expression of Jesus, the next I would act like I had never received His life at all. Roller-coaster Christianity! But even then the times when God expressed Himself through me were exciting!

By hook or by crook, man is out to be like God. The problem is, *How*? Satan convinced Eve that she could make it under her own power. And all false religion (including some religions called Christian) is based on the idea of man being godly by human effort. Haven't you heard someone say, "You have to live the life," or "We Christians must try harder to love our neighbor." Imitating God this way is like a dog walking on his hind legs, or a parrot saying, "Polly wants a cracker." It may be amusing, even amazing, but it is not the real thing.

Suppose a boy wants to become a great baseball player like Mickey Mantle. He attends every game, watches his hero's every step, and doggedly imitates his stance and style. Eventually, he becomes a fairly good baseball player. Who gets the credit? Not Mickey Mantle; he was only the example. It was the boy's effort and the boy will get the contract. Who will get the glory from your life? Is Jesus your example or your life? Is your potential success at godliness dependent upon your ability to imitate, or upon the power of His presence?

> *His divine power has granted to us everything pertaining to life and godliness, through the true knowledge of Him who called us by His own glory and excellence (2 Peter 1:3).*

There is nothing we need to be godly that we do not have when we have His life. That's all it takes, but nothing else will do. In Him is all the love and godliness that exist in the universe. That's why the focus of this verse—2 Peter 1:3—is on Him. These things were granted by His power. There's no other way. His power broke through death and planted the treasure in the clay pot that the world despised. And when the weak things shame the things that are strong (1 Corinthians 1:27), the world knows that the power is of Him and not of ourselves. God wants to show Himself in a way which can only be explained by His presence. Then He will be praised.

Notice that we are not only called to His glory but to His virtue, or goodness, as well. I am amazed how many

Christians, who would never dream of trying to be saved by their own effort, go about attempting to live the Christian life each day by trying to dredge up and utilize some virtue of their own to please God. If they succeed in being kind to another or in avoiding some small temptation, the result is glory to them and a blow to the purpose of God. On the other hand, if they fail, they are plunged into spiritual despondency and self-condemnation because they don't seem able to "live the life." Either way, they are losers!

Among the Christians I associated with in my early Christian life, the custom was to make Sunday evening the occasion for "getting right with God." Many of us would go forward after the regular evening service and pray for forgiveness for all our failures during the previous week. Of course, it didn't seem sincere to pray this way unless it was accompanied by a promise to try harder and do better the next week. And, of course, that never worked. After a while it got harder and harder to ask for forgiveness, and my relationship with Christ became clouded. Once in a while I seemed to break through and was wonderfully aware of the presence of God; but this seemed inevitably followed by a bigger letdown than ever before. This Sunday evening custom is not universal, but the general principle is. I have seen hundreds of Christians living this roller-coaster Christianity. The pity is that eventually a roller-coaster runs down. The peaks get lower until finally there are no peaks anymore and the whole thing just grinds to a halt. And the feeling in the pit of your stomach convinces you that you don't even want to try it again.

The Bible says the key is that we "become partakers of the divine nature" (2 Peter 1:4). And that's the secret! For how could His nature behave other than divinely? Our part is to receive His nature; it is up to His nature to produce the godliness. What more could you ask? More love than He has? More purity than He is?

> *God is not a retailer dispensing grace to us in packets, measuring out some patience to the impatient, some love to the unloving, some meekness to the proud, in quantities that we take and work on as a sort of capital. He has given only one gift to meet all our need: His Son, Christ Jesus.*[1]

Open your Bible right now and look at 1 Corinthians 1:30: "Christ Jesus. . .became to us wisdom from God, and righteousness and sanctification, and redemption." Do you see what it says? We must learn that "Christ is all, and in all" (Colossians 3:11). With His life in our spirit, we can fulfill His purpose. When we learn to live by His life, the result will be the correct balance of spiritual fruit, gifts, and everything else He wants. When Christians come together simply to let Christ be Christ in them, the result will be a spontaneous expression of New Testament church life like our generation has never seen. *Christ is the Christian life.* The question is, Do you know it? "Do you not yourselves realize and know (thoroughly by an ever-increasing experience) that Jesus Christ is in you?" (2 Corinthians 13:5, Amplified Bible).

Jesus said that even He lived by depending on God's life within Him (John 8:28). Then He said, "You shall know the truth, and the truth shall make you free" (John 8:32). Do you want to be free from the terrific bondage of having to keep up a satisfactory performance, and of failing time and time again? The only way is to have and depend upon the Spirit of Christ within your spirit. Yet that is all it takes—just Jesus! With His life present and ready to behave righteously, the pressure is off you! And that is freedom!

In the past couple of years I have had fellowship with several brothers who once served with a Christian organization whose goal was world evangelization. The zeal within this organization had led to a rule that each staff member must witness a certain number of times per week. Reports had to be filed on this by each one. Finally God began to speak to these particular men about what He wanted in their lives. Not long after leaving this organization, one of these men said to me, "It's really great! I'm just beginning to learn to live. I'm discovering what it really means just to be free to be like Christ." I knew he had found what it meant to let Christ be Christ in him. He was learning the spontaneity of being available to God each day for just what God wanted to be in him for that day, and his fruitfulness was increasing.

Another of these fellows shared with me one day the exciting discovery that he had made. He had found that he didn't have to go around with secret cravings lurking beneath the surface all the time. He had found that the resurrection life of Jesus was able to lift him above the problem by replacing it with a wholesome love from God for others. He was free!

> *For if while we were enemies we were reconciled to God through the death of His Son, it is much more [certain], now that we are reconciled, that we shall be saved [daily delivered from sin's dominion] through His [resurrection] life (Romans 5:10, Amplified Bible).*

Freedom! Freedom to live each day above the power of sin's dominion by His life. Freedom because the expression of the life of Jesus is all He is looking for in us. We don't need to provide anything more. In fact, when we do, it is a frustration to God's purpose because it replaces Him in the situation. Anything in the Christian life that does not depend solely on God's supply of His own life is bondage and of no value to God. Everything in church life that does not depend completely on Him is abomination to the Lord. Let's learn to walk and fellowship in the glorious freedom of the saving life of the Lord Jesus Christ. Let's let Him save us from ourselves!

The tragedy of our day is the thousands of Christians

who actually contain the life of God but have not learned to live by it. They try to work out their own salvation, but have never allowed God to work it in (cf. Philippians 2:12-13).

Look around you at the churches, missions, and organizations whose goal is evangelism, who preach Christ, and who are sound in doctrine. Yet many are made of human talents, held together by human constitutions, and supported by human fund-raising. If the Holy Spirit were removed, much of all they do would go on unhindered. While some have done much good, much else is Babel, a tower made by hands with bricks of clay, held together with the mortar of rules and regulations, and plastered with the decoration of attendance numbers and fancy buildings. Countless individual Christians are trying valiantly to live up to their creeds, but in the strength of the human life, just like the heathen next door. And all the time, the life of God lies within trying to express itself, quenched by human nature gone spiritually extroverted. The soul has taken over. The world lies in spiritual darkness, while the light is hid under a bushel of flesh!

Listen to Paul, who had learned the lesson well:

> *I have been crucified with Christ; and it is no longer I who live, but Christ lives in me; and the life which I now live in the flesh I live by faith in the Son of God, who loved me, and delivered Himself up for me. I do not nullify the grace of God; for if righteousness comes through the law, then Christ died needlessly (Galatians 2:20-21).*

This is the "law of the Spirit of life in Christ Jesus" (Romans 8:2). The flesh is out of the way. His life is the life that is being lived. I'm not trying to produce a righteousness of my own by laboring to keep certain laws or standards; I am leaning on Him to be the fulfillment of the requirement of the law in me (see Romans 8:4). I am not trying; I am trusting! We sing so correctly in that little chorus, "He is all I need." He is in me, and I in Him! We are one spirit. The moment I gave my life to be His, His life became mine. He didn't just give His life *for* me; He gave His life *to* me. *And the Christian life is not me living for Him, but Him living through me!*

This is the basic issue of all that God has to say to us and of all that He is doing among us today. If we learn this, we'll have all the rest: we will see the fulfillment of the Great Commission, we will have love among the brethren; we'll have the New Testament pattern in the church simply because it is the most natural wineskin for this kind of wine; we will have the scriptural unity of the church, for when we live by His life, there is nothing left to be sectarian about. Most of the difficulties we encounter in spiritual matters are caused by the constant intrusion of the flesh, the insistence of the human life to express itself for God.

God has made possible an entirely new plane of living for you and me. We are living in an age of unlimited spiritual possibility. It's a great privilege to be in on the "mystery which has been hidden from the past ages and generations; but now has been manifested to His saints, . . .which is Christ in you, the hope of glory" (Colossians 1:26-27). God can make a tremendous impact on our generation through us. But first the clay vessel has to come to the end of itself. We must come to know and experience the insufficiency of our own human life. Only on the ashes of this can God build what He wants in our day. God wants to be God in the twentieth century! Let the flesh step aside so He can begin!

5

BEGINNING BY DYING

If any one wishes to come after Me, let him deny himself, and take up his cross, and follow Me. For whoever wishes to save his life shall lose it; but whoever loses his life for My sake shall find it (Matthew 16:24-25).

I have been crucified with Christ; and it is no longer I who live, but Christ lives in me (Galatians 2:20).

The Christ-life is exciting! There is a freedom, a release, that many never experience. Life is not guilt and bondage but a wonderfully relaxed walk as I simply allow Christ to express Himself. The curse is lifted, God has come in, and that "takes the sweat out of it." This is the truth that makes men free.

But how can I enter into this kind of life? This may surprise you, but the way in is no less than death! God is not looking for a remodeling job but for a new creation. The new life is nothing like the old, and the new man is nothing like the old man. Only the end of the old can bring in the new. We must come to the devastating awareness that "nothing good dwells in me, that is, in my flesh" (Romans 7:8). And out of this must come a heart-desire to die to self.

"Everybody wants to go to heaven, but nobody wants to die." Of course, we're not talking merely about going to heaven but about living *today* as well. Still, the old saying fits, for the conditions are the same. Man has thousands of ways to substitute forms of self-expression and self-seeking for God. Every one of these must slip beneath the sod. But, oh, how we hang on! Little idols limiting God, so that years after becoming Christians, some people still continue to act contrary to the nature of Christ. How much glory could be seen if they would simply come to the end of themselves!

We are sent as Jesus was sent, to be an expression of the life of God in this world. Jesus was "the exact representation of His nature" (Hebrews 1:3). He was not a restriction of God; He was able to say, "He who has seen Me has seen the Father" (John 14:9). Here at last was a man who expressed God as man was intended to do. What was at the root of this extraordinary life?

> *Then Jesus said to His disciples, "If any one wishes to come after Me, let him deny himself, and take up his cross and follow Me" (Matthew 16:24).*

Sounds tough, but Jesus had set the pace. Jesus dreaded the cross, but He denied Himself the choice. "Not My will, but Thine be done" (Luke 22:42). So when He said "follow Me," the response had to be, "I have been crucified with Christ; and it is no longer I who live" (Galatians 2:20) for "the world has been crucified to me, and I to the world" (Galatians 6:14). Jesus demands an attitude that makes us, His disciples, willing to turn our backs on our own lives, give up our own ambitions, and desire to die! And die we must, for "those who are in the flesh cannot please God" (Romans 8:8).

THE SYSTEM

When Adam was cast out of the garden to begin to live by soul-life, he and his children began to establish a system of life which suited them. This system required no faith, no spirit, no God. To live in the system, all man had to do was develop his soul-life so that he could do to his neighbor before his neighbor did to him. When John wrote, "Do not love the world" (1 John 2:15), he was not referring to the planet Earth, but to this system instigated by Satan and perpetuated by man.

The system of men is not the sytem of God. Like water and oil, they don't mix. We must die to the world-system.

Do not love the world, nor the things in the world. If any one loves the world, the love of the Father is not in him. For all that is in the world, the lust of the flesh and the lust of the eyes and the boastful pride of life, is not from the Father, but is from the world (1 John 2:15-16).

The word *lust* here doesn't have the Hollywood meaning of brutish, uncontrollable passions but simply means desire. These desires are common to all human souls and are directly related to the ability of the soul-life to act without God.

The lust, or desire, of the eye is wanting "things" in soulish independence from God. Here's what Jesus said about it.

If anyone wishes to come after Me, let him deny himself, and take up his cross daily, and follow Me. For whoever wishes to save his life [lit., soul-life] shall lose it, but whoever loses his life [soul-life] for My sake, he is the one who will save it. For what is a man profited if he gains the whole world, and loses or forfeits himself? (Luke 9:23-25).

Remember Lot's wife. Whoever seeks to keep his life [soul-life] shall lose it, and whoever loses his life [soul-life] shall preserve it alive (Luke 17:32-33).

There it is! The very act or thought of putting material things before God is of the flesh. Follow Lot's wife and you'll forfeit yourself! But the "system" says, "You need these things; you have a right to them." Jesus replies, "Your heavenly Father knows that you need all these things. But seek first His kingdom, and His righteousness; and all these things shall be added to you" (Matthew 6:32-33). Your Father is concerned about your soul and it needs. But don't jump the gun and lose it all. Let the soul submit its desires to the Spirit and God will supply!

The "lust" or "desire of the flesh" is the ability of the

soul to enjoy apart from God. Jesus hits it hard at its highest expression:

He who loves father or mother more than Me is not worthy of Me; and he who loves son or daughter more than Me is not worthy of Me. And he who does not take his cross and follow after Me is not worthy of Me. He who has found his life [soul-life] shall lose it, and he who has lost his life [soul-life] for My sake shall find it (Matthew 10:37-39).

The "lust of the flesh" is not always sex. Here, it's just overdeveloped sentimental affections which have come before the Lord. Of course, God commands us to love our wives, honor our parents, and so on. When the human life submits to the Spirit, the indwelling Christ will always show the right balance of love of God and love of others. But first, put it in the hands of God. Cling to your own, and you'll lose what you are.

Sometimes the desire of the flesh expresses itself more grossly. We see it, for example, in the raw sex exploitation around us. And it will be seen in the future as the people of the world rally around a man called Antichrist. And, unfortunately, we also see it now in religion, as many believers run from one leader to another, looking for help and answers they should be getting from the Lord. Many are spiritually retarded because the one they followed was also retarded. Many have fallen when the "great leader" they gave all to follow toppled.

But the system's most dangerous and subtle weapon is the "boastful pride of life." Before things and even before people, most of all I love *me*. Haven't you ever felt that you're the only one who really appreciates yourself?

Truly, truly, I say to you, unless a grain of wheat falls into the earth and dies, it remains by itself alone; but if it dies, it bears much fruit. He who loves his life [soul-life] loses it; and he who hates his life [soul-life] in this world shall keep it to life eternal (John 12:24-25).

This time, we're not talking about seeking or finding the

soul-life, but about loving it. That little grain of wheat, so high on the stalk, with its beautiful golden shell, has to drop into the dirty, dark, damp earth. Until then, it's attractive but hard; snug but sterile. You can't tell if there's any life in it or not. But in the earth it dies. The outer coat disintegrates until it is stripped down to reveal the real germ of life within. Then it can begin to bear fruit!

There is a desperate need for men to leave behind the "boastful pride of life" in coming to the Lord Jesus. Today, so many preach: "Just receive Him into your heart. It's easy." Then years later, for some, comes the walk in the Spirit and denial of self-life. Much of modern evangelism declares that the purpose of God is to get men saved and on the way to heaven. No price to pay, nothing to forsake. But that's not His chief purpose and it's not His way.

As I look back, though, I think this was very nearly the approach I took to Christ in the beginning. I was repentant for my past unbelief and gross sins. But I really think I had the idea that I was going to serve God as a Christian disc jockey, go right on living in the same home, add a little church attendance, and give God the wonderful opportunity to use my professional wit and charm for His glory. I know it didn't occur to me that my character was not suitable as it then existed, and I certainly didn't expect any change in income, at least not downward. Christianity was going to be the frosting on an already sweet cake. And then Jesus began to speak to me:

> *Whosoever he be of you that forsaketh not all that he hath, he cannot be My disciples (Luke 14:33, King James Version).*

"All that he hath" doesn't mean only possessions, it means total existence. God is calling men to give up their own soulish existence, their independent lives, their self-seeking goals, ambitions, purposes, and achievements. He is calling us to Himself so that He can be our all in all. That's why *beginning the new life with Jesus means dying to the old one.*

BEGINNING IN THE FIRST CENTURY

Let's drop our own ideas for a moment and go back to the Bible to see how people came to Christ in the first century. The victorious life and church we want depend on the foundation laid in the beginning. We can only get on the right foundation if we are willing to desert any false or shaky ones we have been resting on.

> *For, though by this time you ought to be teachers, you have need again for some one to teach you the elements of the beginning. . .the elementary teaching about the Christ. . .a foundation of repentance from dead works and of faith toward God, of instruction about baptisms, and laying on of hands (Hebrews 5:12; 6:1-2, free translation).*

To become a Christian is to replace an old life with a new one. The elements of the replacement process are spelled out in this passage. The first one is "repentance from dead works." To repent simply means to change your mind and action because you've had second thoughts on the matter. In short, once I discover I am going in the wrong direction, I turn around and follow an entirely new course.

In our case, the first course was all self, living our little human lives with no practical regard for the plan or existence of God. The new course is not just different, it is the opposite! It comes because I had second thoughts about it; I discovered the truth about who I am and what I am for. And I discovered that the essence of my life before was sin against God.

In a nutshell, repentance means that I quit arguing with God about everything and just give up in favor of Him. I am ashamed and sorry, and I am also going to do something about it. I am going to die to self so that I can live unto God.

Without my repentance, God's will for me cannot be realized. Repentance doesn't earn me anything, but it is a condition to salvation because it puts me into a position of being able to fit into God's purpose instead of my own. Repentance is the first "elementary teaching about the Christ."

So repent—change your mind and purpose; turn around and return [to God] that your sins may be erased (blotted out, wiped clean), that times of refreshing. . .may come from the presence of the Lord; and that He may send [to you] the Christ (Acts 3:19-20, Amplified Bible).

Suppose I want to repent, to take a new spiritual direction? The answer is faith!

. . .the elementary teaching about the Christ. . .a foundation of repentance from dead works and faith toward God. . . .

Faith must follow repentance if anything real is to take place. Many have felt sorry enough to want to change—but change to what? Without faith it's simply the same old thing—the flesh, gritting its teeth and trying harder than ever before. The difference between dead works and living works is faith. True repentance leads to complete trust in Jesus.

Believe in the Lord Jesus, and you shall be saved (Acts 16:31).

Paul said this to the jailer at Philippi. But he was not preaching easy-believism! When Paul said this, the man was already very repentant. His world had fallen about his ears, he'd had a change of heart and mind about the whole thing, and he was as ready for the new course of action as he could be. His only question was what should it be. Listen to Paul's answer:

Believe in and on the Lord Jesus Christ—that is, give yourself up to Him, take yourself out of your own keeping and entrust yourself into His keeping, and you will be saved (Acts 16:31, Amplified Bible).

Faith is not just believing that Jesus was; it is trusting Him with all that I am! To believe in Jesus means to believe in Him to the exclusion of everything else! No faith in self, no faith in the flesh, no faith in the "system"—Christ is all!

Well, when the lesson finally began to come, it came hard. Oh, leaving my career was not so tough once I really made the decision. And the house and possessions that went with it dropped off too as the Lord began to change my sense of values. But when I left that city I took self along. I didn't even realize that I was trusting in myself. I planned to go to a Bible college for four years, and I had it all worked out in my mind to get a job in a television station nearby and sail through. I was so confident of the demand for myself that I made the move without even applying for a job. Plenty of time once I get there and get registered for school, I thought.

Then I discovered that my reputation had preceeded me to school. Most of the students were a little younger than I, and with my "glamorous" background, I was soon looked up to as a BMOC (Big Man On Campus). Finally I got around to applying for a job. But God was at work. I couldn't get any job. I tried every radio and television station in miles. Nothing! Finally, a few months later, out of money and desperate, I took a job in a filling station just a few blocks from the school. There I was—Mr. Big Deal—pumping gas in fifty-cent portions for the same students who had thought I was the last word. Lo, how the mighty are fallen. How I hated that job! But looking back, I can see that it was one of the best things that could have happened. Not that it was the total cure. Many more of the same kind of lessons have followed. But it was a beginning. I had to learn that Gary Henley is not the answer, that Jesus is the answer. I'm still learning that in other types of situations today. But I can't help but think that it would have helped if I had known in the beginning, if I had counted the cost before building the tower.

Christ is not limited. But the Christian life can be limited if the foundation is a mixture of Christ and self. If you build a foundation for a one-story house, don't ever try to build a skyscraper on it. It can't take it!

The foundation of the Christian life and church is Christ. That foundation is laid through a deep repentance from sin and self, and through faith that goes far beyond mere "belief" to complete commitment. It involves such a total change from old to new that it is described as "death and resurrection" in the Bible. It would be easier to settle for something less. But the church God is building is made of "living stones" and the foundation has to be solid. Let's lay aside our own ideas and the traditions of men. Build by His plan, for every detail is important when the house is for God.

6

DEAD IN THE WATER

Or do you not know that all of us who have been baptized into Christ Jesus have been baptized into His death? Therefore we have been buried with Him through baptism into death, in order that as Christ was raised from the dead through the glory of the Father, so we too might walk in newness of life (Romans 6:3-4).

Having been buried with Him in baptism, in which you were also raised up with Him through faith in the working of God, who raised Him from the dead (Colossians 2:12).

Let's suppose that I have heard the gospel, that I am really repentant, that I want a new life in Christ more than anything else. What do I do about it?

The answer often is "bow your head and pray, asking Jesus to come into your heart." Now it is entirely possible to find God in this way and thousands have done so, myself included. But the fact remains that this is not the answer given to hungry hearts by the apostles and evangelists of the first century church! And to my knowledge, there is not a single example of anyone coming to God in this way in the entire New Testament. God gave to the early church a step of obedience which was designed to be the "signal" by which a man could say to God, "I am through. I want to die to myself and receive new life in You." That signal is submission to burial by immersion in water baptism.

Now, wait a minute. Don't run away. I'm not talking about baptismal regeneration. I'm not proposing that we replace spiritual rebirth with ritualism. And I'm not ignoring the thief on the cross. Believe me, I know how you feel when you read this. The first time someone pointed this out to me I was so upset I couldn't speak. I then proceeded to think of a good many reasons why it is not so, at least not for today. And all of this in spite of the fact that I had really told the Lord that I would take His Word as my only standard of both faith and practice. "But, Lord, it's just not practical. Nobody else does it that way. People won't respond. Anyway, Lord, You only look on the heart. Salvation is by grace. Baptism is only a symbol, Lord." But the Spirit was wonderfully patient. Slowly the idea began to soak in and the answers began to come. God's ways are better than mine. Let's look at what His Word says about this,

> *. . .a foundation of repentance from dead works and faith toward God, of instruction about baptisms (Hebrews 6:1-2, free translation).*

> *They were pierced to the heart, and said to Peter and the rest of the apostles, "Brethren, what shall we do?" And Peter said to them, "Repent, and let each of you be baptized in the name of Jesus Christ for the forgiveness of your sins" (Acts 2:37-38).*

There is a lot of controversy about baptism. But I think that if you'll just look at all the passages about it without prejudice, you'll come to the conclusion that this is the step God ordained for the man who wants to express repentance and faith. And it's such a perfect step. What could better indicate death, burial, and resurrection? It spells out repentance and faith to the one coming to Christ, to others present, and to God. And it's included in the foundation with repentance and faith.

Now, don't get the idea that baptism is going to earn anybody his salvation. Not at all. Baptism without total trust in Christ will get no one to heaven. But in the New Testament it seems to be the step of obedience which faith demands. It's like an "initiation rite" into a new relationship with Christ, provided that it truly expresses what's in the heart.

Many people get confused about "works" and "faith." Paul says it takes a combination of the two, the "obedience of faith" (Romans 1:5; 16:26). You see, works are dead when there is no faith in them, and faith is dead when there are no works in it (James 2:17). To repent from "dead works" and go on to dead faith would be useless.

Here's an illustration of what I mean. Jesus called Peter to walk to Him on the water (Matthew 14:29). Without faith, Peter could not obey. But without obeying, he could not express faith. If he had stepped out of the boat without faith, he would have sunk like a rock. But, no matter what he said, as long as he stood in that boat he was demonstrating no faith.

> *Only he who believes is obedient, and only he who is obedient believes. For faith is only real when there is obedience, never without it, and faith only becomes faith in the act of obedience.*[1]

The early church understood this. Jesus had told them, "He who has believed and has been baptized shall be saved; but he who has disbelieved shall be condemned" (Mark 16:16). If a man disbelieves there's no point in bringing up baptism. But if he believes, obedience follows!

So when the people cried on the day of Pentecost, "What shall we do?" Peter fired back, "Repent, and let each of you be baptized" (Acts 2:37-38). Their cry showed their belief; now they needed to obey. God would then supply wholeness, forgiveness, and new life. They did exactly what Peter commanded that very day and they were added to the church (Acts 2:41).

This is not a rule for God to obey, but for men to obey. When Peter spoke at Cornelius' house, the Holy Spirit went ahead and fell upon Peter's listeners before he finished (Acts 10:43-48). But Peter didn't try to defend his previous statement, or to object to what God was doing. He just went right ahead and commanded them to be baptized in the name of Jesus Christ. The change was necessary because of the doubt in the Christians' hearts that Gentiles could be saved.

On the road to Damascus, Paul had certainly come to a state of repentance and belief. But he had not received the forgiveness of sins, nor had he been filled with the Holy Spirit (Acts 9:17; 22:16). So Ananias was sent to direct him to the next step:

And now why do you delay? Arise, and be baptized, and wash away your sins, calling His name (Acts 22:16).

And he arose and was baptized (Acts 9:18).

Do you catch the urgency? At Pentecost, the thousands were baptized the same day (Acts 2:4). Cornelius was commanded to be baptized on the spot (Acts 10:47-48). The Philippian jailer was baptized "immediately" (Acts 16:30-33). And now the word of Paul was, "Why do you delay?" (Acts 22:16). Look also at the other accounts in the book of Acts:

But when they believed Philip preaching the good news about the kingdom of God and the name of Jesus Christ, they were being baptized, men and women alike (Acts 8:12).

And Philip opened his mouth, and beginning from this Scripture he preached Jesus to him. And as they went along the road they came to some water; and the eunuch said, "Look! Water! What prevents me from being baptized? And he ordered the chariot to stop; and they both went down into the water, Philip as well as the eunuch; and he baptized him (Acts 8:35-38).

And on the Sabbath day we went outside the gate to a river side, where we were supposing there would be a place of prayer; and we sat down and began speaking to the women who had assembled. And a certain woman named Lydia from the city of Thyatira, a seller of purple fabrics, a worshiper of God, was listening; and the Lord opened her heart to respond to the things spoken by Paul. And when she and her household had been baptized... (Acts 16:13-15).

He said, "Sirs, what must I do to be saved?" And they said, "Believe in the Lord Jesus, and you shall be saved, you and your household." And they spoke the word of the Lord to him together with all who were in his house. And he took them that very hour of the night and washed their wounds, and immediately he was baptized, he and all his household (Acts 16:30-33).

Crispus, the leader of the synagogue, believed in the Lord with all his household, and many of the Corinthians when they heard were believing and being baptized (Acts 18:8).

Paul said, "John baptized with the baptism of repentance, telling the people to believe in Him who was coming after him, that is, in Jesus. And when they heard this, they were baptized in the name of the Lord Jesus" (Acts 19:4-5).

This was standard procedure in the New Testament! Not that the water saved them, of course. But it seems that the act of going down into the water became a sort of point of contact, a point at which faith was released. At this point God moved in and gave spiritual reality to the experience of death and resurrection.

Today much the same thing is happening, as God's people return to this New Testament way. I know of a worker among the Indians in Canada who has baptized in this way for several years. Those being baptized expect God to really meet them and He does. They are often not only forgiven and born again, but baptized with the Spirit as well and come out of the water speaking in tongues and prophesying. The same thing has been the regular experience of a church in California, and also of many other individuals and groups. I know a brother who met two young men on a beach in California, shared Christ with them, and baptized them right there in the ocean. Together the three of them spent the night preaching the gospel to the gathering crowd on the route of the Rose Bowl parade. God has not changed, but how we have limited Him by our unbelief and lack of obedience.

Also notice that when households are mentioned as being baptized, the passage also shows that the members of that household were old enough to hear and believe. The New Testament meaning of baptism has no connection at all with the practice of infant baptism. Baptism which is not accompanied by repentance and faith is not baptism at all!

Sometimes baptism is called "an outward symbol of an inward work already done." Read the passages at the beginning of this chapter again and you'll see that baptism is much more than just a good "symbol" of burial. It does take an inward work of the Spirit to join us to Christ, but it seems that the ideal is for that to take place at the time of baptism.

> *In the days of Noah, during the construction of the ark, in which a few, that is, eight persons, were brought safely through the water. And corresponding to that, baptism now saves you: not the removal of dirt from the flesh, but an appeal to God for a good conscience—through the resurrection of Jesus Christ (1 Peter 3:20-21).*

If you'll stop and think about it, I think you'll see that what the Scripture suggests here is not so very different from what many of us have known and experienced in the past. The same attitudes of heart and mind are required of man, and God must follow through with the same activity of the Holy Spirit if that man is to become truly a new creature in Christ Jesus. And there is always some step which man must take to make that faith and repentance known to God, to personally respond to God's love and to receive God's forgiveness and presence. The question is simply, What do the examples and teaching of the early church tell us that step is? The answer, I believe, is baptism, rather than a prayer of acceptance or something like that. And baptism only saves in the sense that prayer saves: It is the means of appeal to God for new life. It appears to me that God has honored both in experience, but that His Word clearly indicates baptism as the divinely ordained way.

There are a couple of other things I want to mention about baptism. One is that some people are afraid to accept this idea of baptism because they think it damns all the believers, past and present, who were not correctly baptized. I don't believe this is so. Many have found Christ without baptism. Just remember that God holds us responsible only for the light we have and are able to obey. The thief on the cross could not have been baptized. Many others have been taught incorrectly. To damn someone because he does not know God's command concerning baptism or could not obey it would be unjust—and God is just!

On the other hand, God is restoring truth today which has been lost for generations. The important thing is not for you and me to judge others, but to be sure we ourselves are not living by the tradition of men. We want continually to adjust our lives to each word from God. And we want to lead others into new life with Christ in the most scriptural way. I was baptized several months after I came to Christ, but I would not normally lead another to Him today that way. Let's live and work God's way and take care not to set aside details which are important to Him.

The other thing I want to mention is the name in which men are to be baptized. Jesus told His disciples to baptize men "in the name of the Father and the Son and the Holy Spirit" (Matthew 28:19). But the book of Acts tell us that they always baptized in the name of Jesus. Why?

For one thing, the emphasis is not on the words being said but on what is happening. People were baptized, not just *in* the name, but *into* the name of Jesus (Acts 8:16). They were taking on that name as their own, to bear and use in all its authority.

Jesus said to baptize into "the name [singular] of the Father and the Son and the Holy Spirit." What is this name? In the Old Testament, the great revealing name of God was Jehovah. It is used more than 7,000 times to declare who He is. The Holy Spirit is called "the Spirit of Jehovah" (Judges 11:29, etc.). And the name *Jesus* literally means "Jehovah is salvation." The name of the Godhead can be stated as "Jehovah Savior." Therefore, baptizing in the name of Jesus is obeying Matthew 28:19, not contradicting it.

> *And there is salvation in no one else; for there is no other name under heaven that has been given among men, by which we must be saved (Acts 4:12).*

> *Therefore also God highly exalted Him, and bestowed on Him the name which is above every name, that at the name of Jesus every knee should bow (Philippians 2:9-10).*

> *And whatever you do in word or deed, do all in the name of the Lord Jesus, giving thanks through Him to God the Father (Colossians 3:17).*

But what about some of the problems that arise if we follow the Bible pattern for baptism? For instance, aren't there times when it is impossible, or at least very inconvenient? I suppose there might be a few situations in which it would not be possible to baptize someone for forgiveness of sins. If that is absolutely the case, I think I would pray with the individual and plan to follow through with baptism as soon as possible. But when someone really means business, it is amazing how the impossible turns to the possible. Just a few weeks ago we baptized a young man in a small lake near my home when the temperature was about thirty degrees.

I have known some to break holes in the ice to baptize. One group in the Chicago area sometimes baptize new believers in the swimming pool of a motel belonging to one of the elders.

If it's possible, I personally prefer to baptize out-of-doors in some setting of nature. Most groups meeting in homes would not have special facilities for baptism as an organized church would, and these are not necessary. I certainly am not in favor of such groups going to an established church and asking the use of their facilities. But these aspects are not critical. The important thing is that we bring men to God in the way God has decreed. Let's trust Him to make a way.

Another question for many is, Should I be rebaptized? As I've already mentioned, baptism which is without faith and repentance is not really baptism at all. If you were baptized before you really understood the meaning of turning to Christ in spirit and truth, then you should be baptized in reality now that you do understand.

If you were baptized at or after the time when you truly turned to Christ, you may question whether it needs to be done again if you feel it didn't have real spiritual significance for you at the time, or if it was not done in the name of Jesus. Personally, I feel these are decisions that must be reached by each individual in prayer and by seeking guidance from the Spirit. Not everyone will come to the same conclusion; at least, so it seems to me at this time. But for those who desire to be rebaptized, it can have real meaning.

We'll have more to say in chapter 15 on the matter of who should or may baptize. But for now, let me say that there seems to be no biblical reason why any baptized male believer can not baptize anyone else. We have found real meaning in several doing it together as an expression of the body of Christ in operation, rather than assigning the privilege exclusively to one individual.

The essential thing in all of this is that we see where

baptism fits into the overall plan of God for us. God has a great thing in mind and it can't be lightly approached. It requires new men, and that means the old man has to come to the end by death. The way God asks us to submit to that death is to submit to water baptism. It is at this point of repentance, faith, surrender, death and burial that God goes to work in our lives to give us the spiritual experience which will make the new life a reality. Important as it is, our part is by far the smaller part. God's side of the action is what really makes it work! And that's what we'll look at next.

7

SPIRITUAL EXPERIENCE

In Him we have redemption through His blood, the forgiveness of our trespasses (Ephesians 1:17).

Knowing this, that our old self was crucified with Him. . .that we should no longer be slaves to sin (Romans 6:6).

But God. . .made us alive together with Christ (Ephesians 2:4-5).

I am sending forth the promise of My Father upon you; but you are to stay in the city until you are clothed with power from on high (Luke 24:49).

We've been looking at the things which we must do to come to God. These things are necessary and can't be taken lightly. We must repent and believe, and express these by being baptized. So we see clearly that there is a step which is up to us. "Draw near to God and He will draw near to you" (James 4:8).

But it's not what we do but what God does that actually fits us spiritually to know God and to express Him. We are clay vessels—we can be open, but God must fill us with the treasure! That little clay pot must be receptive, but God will have to do the cleansing, the breaking, the molding and the filling. And when He does, the clay pot, with its human soul and human spirit, will experience the activity of God in a very real and personal way. This is what I mean by "spiritual experience."

By "experience" I don't mean just the emotional reaction. I mean the spiritual dealing of God with your inner man. This in itself is an experience which may also produce an emotional response in the soul. The night I turned to Christ

I k*new* I was forgiven and made spiritually alive! I cried like a baby and shook so hard that I nearly rattled the mobile home we were living in at that time. I see nothing wrong in this, though not everyone responds the same way. But these initial emotions passed, and the conscious awareness of forgiveness and life in my spirit continued.

Just what sort of spiritual experience should we expect? Actually, the Christian life is made up of countless occasions of experiencing God at work in our lives. But I am thinking of that which is basic and vital if God is to save us from ourselves for Himself and equip us for His eternal purpose. In other words, I am talking about the spiritual experience of salvation.

I use that term with fear and trembling, because so many people have their own ideas of what it means. To many, it means an escape hatch from hell—we're going to heaven some day. If you've read the first six chapters of this book, you know God has more than that in mind for us. By salvation, I mean all that has been provided for us by Jesus' own experience two thousand years ago.

Salvation is really one thing. But in order to discuss it, we're going to break it down into four parts, or phases. While each of these phases is quite distinctive, we'll see that the New Testament pattern was normally for believers to experience salvation with all of its phases as virtually one experience. But we have to recognize that today people sometimes experience salvation a phase at a time and that others still have not entered into all that God has for them. This frequently occurs because salvation is often proclaimed only in part, so people have faith only for a part as they come to Christ.

The important thing is to see the totality of what God has for us so that we can be fully equipped. It may be that your experience has been only a part of the total. Or it may be that one aspect of salvation was more meaningful for you than another. The human tendency is to form a theology around experience. Those who have done this have often stopped short of God's best.

Let's objectively compare our lives with all that God has provided. If you come to the conclusion that you have not experienced all that God has for you, go to Him and He will meet you in your need and hunger. Remember that we are still coming out of the dark ages. The Holy Spirit is restoring truth that has been largely lost to the church for centuries. We need to stay flexible and to search the Word continually with an open heart, ready to adjust our concepts and our lives when God reveals something we may have missed or misunderstood before.

I think it will clear the air a little if we can see how each phase of basic spiritual experience is directly related to something the Lord Jesus did in providing salvation for us.

1. Shedding of His blood	1. Forgiveness of sins
2. His death	2. Death of the old man
3. His resurrection	3. Eternal life imparted—new man
4. His ascension and exaltation	4. Clothed with power of Spirit

Each part of our experience (right-hand column) is a direct result of the Lord's experience (left-hand column). They are all closely related in both His experience and ours. Yet the fact remains that many people today do not have a living experience of all of these aspects of salvation. I've talked with a number of professing Christians who have no real assurance of being forgiven, and at least as many others who don't have a conscious experience of Jesus Christ living within them. And then there are the thousands who know they are forgiven and born again, but for whom the death of the old man has no meaning in their lives, or who have never had the Spirit come upon them in power for ministry. Let's take a closer look at these phases of salvation and find out where you and I fit in.

FORGIVENESS OF SINS

We're separated from God by our sins. "Your iniquities have separated between you and your God, and your sins have hid his face from you" (Isaiah 59:2). Trying to associate with God in our sins would be like trying to get germs to live in peaceful coexistence with a powerful antiseptic. It can't be done. If we are going to know God personally, we've got to be cleansed from all the guilt and impurity first. This is the purpose of the blood.

This is My blood of the covenant, which is to be shed on behalf of many for forgiveness of sins (Matthew 26:28).

But why is blood necessary? Many people would rather we'd come up with something else, another way. Is it possible? No, for "without shedding of blood there is no forgiveness" (Hebrews 9:22). But, why?

The reason is that the blood of man contains man's human life. "The life (lit., soul) of the flesh is in the blood" (Leviticus 17:11; cf. Leviticus 17:14; Genesis 9:4). Man's sin is committed by his soul. So it is the life of the flesh or body (the blood) that has to pay. "For the wages of sin is death" (Romans 6:23) and, "surely your blood, the blood of your lives, will I require" (Genesis 9:5).

God is just. With Him, judgment and penalty always follow transgression. Anything less would be compromise. I'm amazed how many people refuse to see this about God. They want a weak, wishy-washy God who, because of His love, can't bear to punish sin. Can you imagine the shock if these same people called the police to arrest a lawbreaker and were told to simply overlook it and love the criminal? Order in either government or the universe demands that sin must have a wage, a penalty.

But the good news of amazing grace is that God has allowed and even provided a substitute to pay the penalty for us. The substitute is His own Son Jesus, and the penalty was the shedding of His blood.

But God demonstrates His own love for us, in that while we were yet sinners, Christ died for us. Much more then, having now been justified by His blood, we shall be saved from the wrath of God through Him (Romans 5:8-9).

A great illustration of this is in Exodus 12. The death angel was coming and only one thing could save a household: the blood of the passover lamb. This was placed on the doorposts outside the home, for God had said, "When I see the blood, I will pass over you" (Exodus 12:13). God had demanded the blood and God was satisfied when He saw it. We need to see that God is satisfied and demands nothing more. No wonder I shook and cried! The life of His Son has been poured out; what could be added to that? On this basis we are forgiven. It was done completely by "Him who loves us, and released us from our sins by His blood" (Revelation 1:5). And that's all it takes, because "the blood of Jesus His Son cleanses us from all sin" (1 John 1:7).

This is where the experience comes in. Each Christian needs to really know that he is forgiven. Doubts must go. One college student I saw turn to Christ said, "Wow, man. It's really gone, isn't it! I feel like I've just been unchained from a big steel ball of sin." The Bible says, "We have confidence to enter the holy place by the blood of Jesus" (Hebrews 10:19). We can come into the presence of God without fear when we know that He sees the blood and we are forgiven.

Guilt is the main hangup of our generation. It's not for believers! We need to know with our hearts as well as with our heads that we are clean in His sight.

It has to be the experience of your life that no past sin, no matter how gross, is held against you. And you have to know, as you continue in the Christian life, that each time you come to God it is on the same basis—not, Have I done well or not—but, I have been cleansed by His blood.

There are two basic ways your fellowship with God can be interrupted and your Christian life messed up. One way occurs when you don't walk in the Spirit and sin creeps into your life. Not necessarily anything big, but still sin. Soon your relationship with the Lord is like owing somebody an overdue debt. Tension builds, and you start avoiding him. Do you ever feel this in your relationship to God? Like something has come between you? It may be true. If it is, the blood is the answer.

This was a very big problem for me in my early Christian life. When I sinned, I would sense the alienation, but I didn't know what to do about it. I would begin instinctively to avoid God, cutting out devotions, and so forth. Then I found I would grow weaker and have even less power to overcome sin. The result was that I would sin again, and round and round I went. I can't begin to tell you how it helped me to learn that I don't ever have to be consciously estranged from uninhibited fellowship with God. The blood covers it all if I'll just take advantage of His provision!

If we confess our sins, He is faithful and just to forgive us our sins and to cleanse us from all unrighteousness (1 John 1:9).

The blood of Jesus His Son cleanses us from all sin (1 John 1:7).

Just go to the Lord Jesus and honestly confess. (The word *confess* means to agree with God about it.) There is nothing you can do to repay God or make up for your sin, although He may require confession and restitution if you have offended another. But as you repent and confess in faith, He will forgive you and cleanse you by His blood just as He did in the beginning.

The other way occurs when the devil tries to condemn you falsely. He is called "the accuser of the brethren." From time to time, he will try to drag up things from your past life and convince you that they are not really forgiven. If you believe him, the effect can be the same as if you had really sinned: guilt! Even though the guilt is not real, if you believe the accusation it can still impair your fellowship with God. The answer? The blood! "The accuser of our brethren has been thrown down. . . .They overcame him because of the blood of the Lamb" (Revelation 12:10-11). Just stand right up to him and tell him: "I rebuke you, Satan! You have no right to accuse me. I belong to Jesus and His blood has covered all my sin. In the name of Jesus I take authority over you and forbid you to accuse me any more." The devil loses his place as accuser when we know experientially that we are cleansed and forgiven by the blood of Jesus!

When can I know this experience of total forgiveness is mine? Ideally, at the point when faith and repentance are expressed in baptism. "Repent and let each of you be baptized in the name of Jesus Christ for the forgiveness of your sins" (Acts 2:38). "Arise, and be baptized, and wash away your sins" (Acts 22:16). This was the normal pattern in the New Testament. Today, others have experienced it at another time, perhaps before baptism. But it must be the experience of your own life, or you'll never be able to move on to be conformed to the image of Jesus, which is God's purpose for your life.

THE DEATH OF THE OLD MAN

God has dealt with what we have done with the *blood* of Jesus. But He has also dealt with what we are by the *death* of Jesus. Let me explain. The Bible refers to sins, but it also speaks of sin. Sin is the principle of independence from God. When this principle becomes active in a man, he sins. Sins (murder, adultery, etc.) are the result of sin, not the cause. They are like the symptoms of a disease. You know a child has measles when you see the spots. But the doctor doesn't treat the spots, he treats the problem within. God removes the "spots" (our sins) by the blood of Jesus. But if He stopped there the "spots" would come right back because the inner problem had not been treated. God's solution is not simply to remove the sins. The old man who is a slave to the principle of independence from God must be removed from the scene. Only then can something more positive begin.

Remember that *old man* is a term the Bible uses to describe the entire nature of the natural man. It is not just some part of him, some little darkened corner of his mind or heart that needs to be removed. It is the old man himself who is in God's way.

The old man is what he is because it was all his father had to pass on to him. All the way back to Adam, his ancestors were missing something. "Through one man's [Adam's] disobedience the many were made sinners" (Romans 5:19). When I chose to live in Chicago, I chose for my children. When Adam chose to live without the Spirit, he chose for me. When Adam sinned, I was "in him"; just as when my grandfather homesteaded in South Dakota, I was in him. If he had died before marrying, where would I be? This is my problem with Adam. All that I am is tied up in the fact that I am in his family. And that whole family is missing something. Now, there is nothing I can do about my family background, but there is something God can do:

By His doing you are in Christ Jesus (1 Corinthians 1:30).

God solved the problem of my connection with Adam by giving me a new family background, a new ancestry. When God placed me in Christ, He gave me a "retroactive contract." He dated it all the way back to Jesus' death. I am now in Jesus' family, not Adam's. So whatever happened to Jesus happened to me—I was there. Paul says, "Our old self was crucified with Him" (Romans 6:6). My family line has been changed from Adam to Christ. Since this goes back two thousand years, everything that happened to Him happened to me, too. Watchman Nee uses the illustration of a piece of paper placed in a book.[1] What ever happens to the paper. Mail the book and you mail the paper; destroy the book and you destroy the paper. Romans 6:6 shows us how this helps us today:

Knowing this, that our old man was crucified with Him, that our body of sin might be made inactive, that we should no longer be a slave to sin (free translation).

This verse mentions three things:

1. Sin: the principle of independence from God.
2. The old man: with a dead spirit he was always independent from God, so he was a slave to sin.
3. Body of sin: the physical body which carried the old man's independence into action—sin became sins.

Sin, as a principle, is still in the world. But God solved the problem by getting rid of the one who always had to obey it and by replacing him with a new man. When that happened, you might say that the body "lost its job" of sinning. It retired from that occupation to do better things. I am a new man and neither I nor any part of me is a slave to sin. I don't have to obey sin, even though as a principle it still exists in the world. My body and I can obey the Spirit of God within instead and do godly things instead of commit sins.

The problem is that so many Christians don't see this and have never experienced it. They say, "After all, we're still sinners, you know. The old man is still with us. Well, everybody sins."

Many believers live daily lives of fear, awaking in the morning with the conviction that they will surely sin today, no matter what. To them, it's a part of life, a necessary evil. Prepared to fail, they usually do, and this strengthens their convictions even more. After all, they "tried so hard" and look what happened. It never occurs to them to follow the simple scriptural principle of relying on the life of Christ within rather than their own effort. It never strikes them that they really are no longer slaves to sin.

This doesn't mean that it's not possible for a Christian to act in the flesh and sin. But it does mean that he always has the potential of trusting Christ, obeying God, and defeating sin. Someone said, "It's not that I'm not able to sin; it's that

I'm able not to sin!" The only one who has to sin is the old man, and, praise God, he is dead!

> *Such deliverance God provides for every believer; all may enter in. Moreover, let us be unmistakenly clear that this liberation from the power of sin may be experienced the very hour a sinner accepts the Lord Jesus as Saviour and is born anew. He need not be a longtime believer and undergo numerous defeats before he can receive this gospel. Delay in accepting the gospel according to Romans 6 is due either to the incomplete gospel he has heard or to his unwillingness in wholly accepting and yielding to it. Whereas actually this blessing should be the common possession of all the newly born.*[2]

The Bible says, "Even so consider yourselves to be dead to sin, but alive to God in Christ Jesus" (Romans 6:11). This is not a matter of considering harder, but of simply knowing what God has done and accepting it. This faith attitude should have led us to the experience at baptism, but if not, the way is clear. One brother who has been a Christian for years really only saw this for the first time while reviewing the early copies of this manuscript. While reading, the Spirit made it real; he believed, and now testifies to a real change in his life as a result. The Word of God is the only basis for faith, and the Word says it has been done; the old man was crucified. Let's believe it and proclaim it! And let's live triumphantly because of it!

8

SPIRITUAL EXPERIENCE (*Continued*)

But God. . .made us alive together with Christ (Ephesians 2:4-5).

I am sending forth the promise of My Father upon you; but you are to stay in the city until you are clothed with power from on high (Luke 24:49).

THE RESURRECTION LIFE OF THE NEW MAN

So far we've been looking at the negative side of the gospel. Now we come to the exciting, positive side. We've seen how God has removed, first, the guilt of sins and, second, the old man himself. Now He will create the new man and give to him the life and power of the Spirit.

Therefore we have been buried with him through baptism into death, in order that as Christ was raised from the dead through the glory of the Father, so we too might walk in the newness of life. Even so consider yourselves to be dead to sin, but alive to God in Christ Jesus (Romans 6:4, 11).

The secret is still the fact that we are in Christ and in His experience: in the shedding of His blood for forgiveness; in His death for the end of the old man; and now, in His resurrection so that we can have new life! And the life we receive is His own eternal, uncreated life! This is what makes a new man—sharing in the resurrection life of Jesus. This is why we were created, clay pots, containers for the life of Jesus!

It's an amazing thing—really two births and two deaths! Born alive in the flesh, but dead to God; we have to die to sin and self and be born of the Spirit alive to God. No wonder religion can't do it. It's a miracle of God as great as all creation. In fact, it's called a creation in the Bible:

For neither is circumcision anything, nor uncircumcision, but a new creation (Galatians 6:15).

Therefore if any man is in Christ, he is a new creation (2 Corinthians 5:17, RSV).

The new man is a new creation of God! He has an entirely new source and center of his life, a living spirit, merged with God's Spirit, containing "everything pertaining to life and godliness" (2 Peter 1:4). His soul, freed from sin and yielded to the Spirit, is being transformed. And his body, because it is now the possession of God and is the tabernacle of the Spirit, will one day be glorified. He is a new man, part of a new race, born into a new family, living a new life, singing a new song. He has a new potential and a new purpose—to express the life of God in this world.

In explaining this, I sometimes use the illustration of the caterpillar. He's an ugly, hairy little worm who was created to fly in the heavens but is restricted to a slow crawl in the dirt. Then one day he creeps into a cocoon and "dies." Then he is "born again" and comes out a beautiful butterfly. In a way, he is the same little fellow who went in, but in another way he is completely different. Now he soars in the heavens and spreads beauty over the earth. Nothing could have done this for him but death and birth. No flying school, no paper wings, no amount of positive thinking could have made that little worm fly; it took a rebirth!

I once shared this illustration in a ladies meeting where I was speaking. Several months later I was in another meeting and a lady came up and introduced herself by saying, "Hello, I'm Natalie. I'm a butterfly. And have I ever been flying!" She went on to tell how she had committed her life to Jesus Christ and how her husband had done the same a few weeks later. She was one of the most radiant people I have ever met! Changed by the power of God!

Peter says we are "born again to a living hope through the resurrection of Jesus" (2 Peter 1:3). This is a far cry from a "pray for me that I'll hold out to the end" kind of Christianity! Part of our hope is for heaven, but Peter also says that the result of this birth is that we might be "like the Holy One who called you" (2 Peter 1:15). We have received more than Adam ever did, and we need to know it, believe it, and walk in it. I can't think of a more exciting way to live!

Paul's prayer was that he might experience "the power of His resurrection" (Philippians 3:10). Many people who have been born again don't experience the power of resurrection life in daily living. And there are plenty of others who agree doctrinally but have never actually been made alive in Christ. The new birth is not just an emotional experience, but neither is it just a shift to a more orthodox doctrine without a real experience with the Spirit. This seems to be all that some people have.

Remember too that when you're born, you still have to grow. The life you received is perfect but not yet mature. New life is not full grown; it has to ripen and mature like fruit. The possibilities of the new life are staggering. The Holy Spirit is able to bring the new man into complete victory. But there must be development "until Christ is formed in you" (Galatians 4:19).

> *The new [man] which in the likeness of God has been created in righteousness and holiness of the truth (Ephesians 4:24).*

> *The new [man]. . .is being renewed to a true knowledge according to the image of the One who created him (Colossians 3:10).*

There is a beginning and a process. A creation in the image of God, and then a time of renewal and of being conformed fully to Him. Either one without the other falls short of what God wants. But the creation comes first. We're going to look a lot more closely at the matter of living as a new man in th next chapter. But for now, let's move on to the final phase of spiritual experience.

THE NEW MAN CLOTHED WITH POWER FOR MINISTRY

As wonderful as he is, the new man is still not equipped to fulfill God's purpose until he is clothed with the power of the Holy Spirit as well. There is a lot of confusion about this operation of the Spirit today, and I want to try to clear up some of it for you. Just remember that God doesn't always arrange things in the Bible into the neat little categories that would satisfy the minds of modern men. The experience of Cornelius, for example, is a living thing, not a chapter in a systematic theology book. Reading about him today, each of us tends to interpret his experience in the light of our own. That's a natural thing to do, but if it only strengthens our preconceived opinions rather than moving us forward spiritually, it's not good.

Part of the confusion concerning the work of the Spirit is the fact that we sometimes don't agree in our terminology. For instance, to the average fundamentalist, "receiving the Spirit" means the experience in which the Spirit first comes to dwell within to give new life—spiritual birth, in other words. But to the average Pentecostalist, the same term means an experience of receiving the Spirit in His ministry of baptizing with power for witnessing. Each can find grounds in the Scripture for his use of the term. But I can't think how many times I have seen some excited brother, who had just been introduced to this additional phase of the Spirit's work, try to share it with another, and have it end in discord and division. Many times, it was just because the second brother thought the first was saying that he did not in any way have the Spirit of God in him. Of course he was turned off; he thought his friend was saying that he was not even a real Christian.

It has helped me a great deal to realize the different aspects of the Spirit's work. If anyone has been born again, the Holy Spirit has come into his spirit to give him new life. The Bible says, "If anyone does not have the Spirit of Christ, he does not belong to Him" (Romans 8:9). But it is possible to have the Spirit within, and still not have had Him come upon me to equip me with power to share Christ with the outside world.

The indwelling of the Spirit is linked to the resurrection of Jesus and is that which gives us new life in our inner man. This is "Christ in us, our only hope," the way we become "partakers of the divine nature." The indwelling Spirit produces the fruit of the Spirit within so our lives can always be expressions of the nature of Jesus, no matter what the world throws at us.

On the other hand, the Spirit clothing me with power is a result of the exaltation of Jesus and is primarily an outward thing to help me communicate the truth and power of God to others, both believers and unbelievers. In other words, this is power for witnessing. Along with power for witnessing comes, not so much the fruit, but the gifts of the Spirit. Both the fruit and the gifts of the Spirit make an impact on others, but the fruit is primarily an inner work of the Spirit to make us like Him, whereas the gifts are primarily without and serve to build up others spiritually. (See I Corinthians 12:7, 14:26).

Let's look at the way it began on the day of Pentecost. Peter is speaking:

> *This Jesus, God raised up again, to which we are all witnesses. Therefore having been exalted to the right hand of God, and having received from the Father the promise of the Holy Spirit, He has poured forth this which you both see and hear. Therefore let all the house of Israel know for certain that God has made Him both Lord and Christ—this Jesus whom you crucified (Acts 2:32-33, 36).*

The things the crowd saw and heard on the day of Pentecost were the direct result of Jesus being exalted. In one sense His work was not completed at His death or even at His resurrection, but only when He had been seated at the right hand of the Father and had poured forth the Holy Spirit in power (Acts 2:33). Only then could the world be evangelized and churches planted. For these things have to be done by Christians who are clothed with the power of the Spirit.

This is why Jesus told His followers to wait in the city and not do any work until the Spirit came upon them (Luke 24: 49). The waiting was not because they were not fit to be empowered, but because He was not yet exalted. Now the wait is over—He is Lord—and we can and should be clothed with power to be His witnesses in the world.

Luke tells us that when Jesus told them to go as witnesses, He spoke of the necessity of being clothed with the power of the Spirit. In Mark, when He said, "Go," (Luke 16:15), He also said, "and these signs will accompany those who have believed" (Luke 16:17). The Bible tells us that "they went out and preached everywhere, while the Lord worked with them, and confirmed the word by the signs that followed" (Luke 16:20). Today there is a lot of preaching and little power, because many know Him as the indwelling Spirit but are not clothed with His power.

Maybe an illustration will help you to understand this better. I once saw a man trying to direct traffic in the middle of a busy intersection in Chicago's Loop. He was wearing an ordinary business suit, and he was having a terrible time. Nobody was doing what he told them to do. He seemed as big and as strong as the policeman who usually stood in that intersection, and he may even have been authorized by the police department to be there. But the fact remains that he was unable to communicate that strength and authority to others because he was not properly clothed. We may have the strength of Christ within and go in the authority of His name, but we need to be clothed with the power of the Spirit to minister to others.

Of course, the policeman needs more than a uniform. He needs to eat a good breakfast before he begins the day so he will have the inner strength for his job. But eating a good breakfast won't help much if he forgets his uniform. On the other hand, wearing the uniform won't help much if he gets too weak to stand in the intersection. Both are necessary. I have seen many believers who have Christ within and express the fruit of the Spirit, but lack power to communicate spiritual things to others. Then I have seen some others who are clothed with power and manifest gifts, but who have not learned to live by His life within and who lack the grace and love to glorify His name. We need the Spirit of God within *and* upon us to fulfill God's purpose for our lives.

Another term which is sometimes used in the Bible to describe this experience is "baptism with the Spirit." Again, this term has been the cause of some confusion, but it doesn't have to. Jesus said, "You shall be baptized with the Holy Spirit not many days from now. . . .You shall receive power when the Holy Spirit has come upon you; and you shall be My witnesses" (Acts 1:5-8). The promise was fulfilled on the day of Pentecost after His exaltation.

The problem centers in the interpretation of 1 Corinthians 12:13: "By one Spirit we were all baptized into one body." Is this the same baptism referred to by John in Matthew 3:11? "He who is coming after me is mightier than I, and I am not even fit to remove His sandals; He Himself will baptize you with the Holy Spirit and fire." It seems to me that the word *baptism* is being applied descriptively in these two passages to two distinct aspects of God's work in the believer's life. In Corinthians, Paul speaks of the Spirit as the one doing the baptizing, and that into which we are baptized (plunged or placed) is the body of Christ. But in Matthew, Jesus is spoken of as the one doing the baptizing and He does it by enveloping us in the presence of the Spirit which Christ is pouring out upon us. In other words, one spiritual baptism is a plunging into the body, while the other is an outpouring upon us.

Further complicating the issue is the fact that in New Testament experience, both of these baptisms probably occurred simultaneously with water baptism, though perhaps not always. The important thing is to see that both experience and Scripture teach us that it is possible to be included in the body of Christ, but still not be clothed with the power of the Holy Spirit from on high. And above all, don't let these technical aspects distract you from the wonderful truth that God is showing us in the term *baptism with the Spirit.*

I've heard many people refer to "receiving the baptism." This is incorrect. We do not "receive the baptism"; we are baptized with the Spirit so that we can be clothed, or covered, with His power. Let me illustrate. Take a water glass and put some water in it. You would say that it has "received" water within. But next "baptize" that glass by pouring out upon it the contents of a five-gallon bucket of water. Now the glass is not only filled within, but overflowing and covered with water outside as well. So it is when the Spirit baptizes us and clothes us with power.

Can I know if the Spirit has come upon me in this way? If so, how? First, because the Spirit coming upon me is an experience, it can't take place without me knowing it. I have met a great many people who have been baptized with the Spirit, and though their experiences were often varied, they all knew what had taken place. My own experience included being caught up in an hour or so of the purest and most concentrated worship I have ever known. I was in a room with about two hundred other people; yet I stood for an hour, hands upraised, caring only about the fact that the presence of God was flooding my entire being. I have never been so aware of the presence of God. I have read the testimonies of men like Moody, Finney, Torrey, and others who seem to have had similar experiences. In some ways they varied, but the central fact is that we were all *experiencing* what God was doing!

Second, I have discovered that it is at the point of being clothed with the power of the Spirit that we also are able to enter into the gifts of the Spirit. Ephesians 4:7-8 shows that the bestowal of gifts upon the church was the result of Jesus being exalted, just as was the Spirit being poured out. The gifts are a part of the means God uses to communicate spiritual things to men, both to believers and unbelievers. That is why you can't have real New Testament evangelism without the power of the Spirit and the gifts. And neither can you have a scriptural gathering of the local church. I have seen many instances of people who have seen the truth of the ministry of the body of Christ one to another, but who have come together to try to do this without the gifts of the Spirit. At best, they have a glorified Bible discussion—but that is not a New Testament church meeting. I want to share more about the gifts later, but for now it's enough to say that the gifts are available as the Spirit comes upon us in power and this is one of the ways we may know when we are baptized with the Spirit.

The normal manifestation when the Spirit comes upon men is speaking in tongues. There are reasons for this. One is that tongues can not only be used to edify others (with interpretation) (1 Corinthians 14:5), but it can also edify the person speaking the tongue in personal spiritual conversation with God (1 Corinthians 14:2,4). I can't think of anything that has done more for my prayer life than "praying in the Spirit." God is sovereign in giving gifts for the edification of others, but I can't believe He would give me a source of personal edification and withhold it from you. Because of this, and also taking into account the frequency of tongues in scriptural accounts and in present-day experience I feel that any Christian who has been baptized and clothed with the power of the Spirit is able to speak in tongues "devotionally" if he wants to.

However, to say dogmatically that one is not baptized with the Spirit unless he speaks in tongues at that time is going further than Scripture does. It was not always true in the early church and it is not always true today. Only three of the five cases in the book of Acts are definitely said to have spoken in tongues at the time the Spirit came upon them (Acts 2:4; 10:46; 19:6). The Samaritans seem to have done something observable, but the Bible doesn't say what it was (Acts 8:16-18). Paul testified to his ability to speak in tongues, but there is no record or indication that this manifestation began when the Spirit initially came upon him (1 Corinthians 14:18; cf. Acts 9:17-18). The disciples at Ephesus both spoke in tongues and prophesied (Acts 19:6). It seems unclear to me whether they all spoke with tongues and then they all prophesied, or whether some people spoke in tongues and others prophesied.

With such a margin for question in the cases of Paul, the Samaritans, and the disciples at Ephesus, it seems unwise to insist that everyone today experience the same manifestation of tongues at the time the Spirit comes upon them.

We have seen several definitely baptized with the Spirit who did not begin to speak with tongues until several days later. One friend had a very real experience of being clothed with the power of the Spirit, with several changes in his life as a result. He didn't speak with tongues until a couple of years later when someone showed him that this was his privilege. Then, by faith, he very simply and easily entered in.

Of course, we also have the testimonies of such men as Moody, Torry, and others whose ministries were profoundly affected by an experience which they themselves described as the baptism with the Spirit. Yet some of these men apparently never did speak with tongues.

I can only conclude that while tongues is often the norm for Spirit-filled believers, we must leave room for those upon whom the Spirit falls but who do not manifest tongues. More charity all around would help a great deal to preserve the unity of the Spirit while talking about the power of the Spirit.

On the other hand, we need to be open individually for all that the Lord may have for us. I know Christians who have decided that they will never speak in tongues and by dictating terms to God have limited or even prevented the Spirit from coming upon them in power. Just recently I talked to a young man who told me that "God has shown me that He loves me and that He won't make me speak in tongues if I don't want to." Well, that certainly is true, but it is a dangerous and limiting position to take. God won't forgive you either if you don't want Him to, but who would be that foolish to turn down a gift offered by God? Don't tell God what to do. If you know that you have been baptized and clothed with the power of the Spirit, yet have not spoken in tongues, simply go to the Lord in faith and ask Him to bring you into this added dimension. Luke 11 assures us that there is no need to fear anything that the Father gives us. We can ask in confidence. Let each one search his own heart and the Word of God prayerfully to be sure that we have allowed God to do a thorough work of preparation.

If your experience does not include being clothed with the power of the Spirit and entering into the spiritual gifts, it may help you to have some others pray for you. This seems to be where the fourth foundation of Hebrews 6:1 figures in:

> *A foundation of repentance from dead works and of faith toward God, of instruction about baptism, and laying on of hands.*

Immediately after baptizing the twelve men at Ephesus, Paul "laid his hands upon them, the Holy Spirit came on them, and they began speaking with tongues and prophesying" (Acts 19:6). Paul also spoke of the spiritual gift which Timothy had received when Paul and the elders laid their hands on him (1 Timothy 4:14; 2 Timothy 1:6). Ask a few believers who have experienced the Spirit's power themselves to gather about you and pray for you with the laying on of their hands, joining their faith to yours that God will pour out His Spirit upon you in power for ministry.

The important thing in all of this is to see that the man God wants is a man well furnished with all God has provided. I need to be forgiven and cleansed from all sin, crucified to sin and self, created a new man with a living spirit, and clothed with the power of the Spirit. Nothing short of this will do. Praise God for those who have entered into each of these things, whether at once or on separate occasions. If you haven't, the provision is there. You don't need to plead or beg, and you can't earn anything from God. Just ask the Spirit to reveal what He has for you and then enter in through faith to the experience of reality.

As for future converts, I really see the need to instruct them with a whole gospel and to believe with them for a full work of the Spirit as we baptize them in water. New Testament Christians are necessary for accomplishing God's purpose and only New Testament evangelism can produce them!

9

LIVING BY FAITH*

It is no longer I who live, but Christ lives in me; and the life which I know live in the flesh I live by faith in the Son of God (Galatians 2:20).

Living! This is where it really counts! And this is where most of us have our real problems. If you're like me at all, you've found that it's one thing to know that your life is to be an expression of God's nature, even to have experienced Him indwelling and empowering you; but it's another thing altogether to go through an average day and experience Him living and loving through you in every situation! In other words, Christ is in me, but how does He come out of me?

The answer is faith. God's purpose is for us to be dependent upon Him so that He can be the source of His own image as seen in us. And that is faith! There is no other way to live the Christian life than by faith. The Bible clearly tells us that "without faith it is impossible to please Him" (Hebrews 11:6). Not difficult: impossible! Impossible because "whatever is not from faith is sin" (Romans 14:23). One of the most basic things we have to learn about the Christian life is that "the righteous man shall live by faith" (Romans 1:17). But what in the world *is* faith? Where do we get it? How do we use it? And why does the whole thing seem so difficult in practice when it looks so simple in theory?

* *If the reader is not reading this book through in one sitting or if he is not quite familiar with the basic concept presented in chapter 4, he will be greatly benefited by quickly reading it before beginning this chapter.*

The big difficulty for most of us is the determination of the flesh, the soulish human life, to try to serve God in its own strength. The big lesson we have to learn is to shift the load, by faith, onto the ability of the life of God within us. I sometimes feel as though I could retire if I had a dime for every time I thought I had completely learned that lesson once and for all. But gradually it is coming.

Don't get discouraged if it takes a while. God has been teaching this same lesson to His people all down through the ages, and it took some of them a long time.

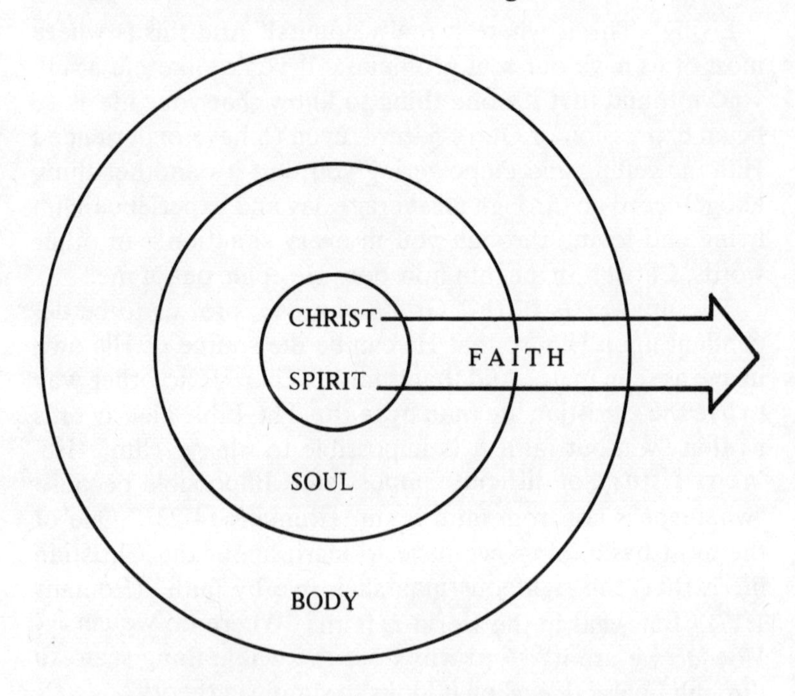

I think the one I have learned the most from is Moses. At the age of forty he was committed to God and had an inner knowledge of what his special mission was to be. But how did he carry out this great divinely assigned task? He got a stick and started to beat the Egyptian army to death, one by one. Of course, he didn't get very far on that project. It was the right man and the right job, but done the wrong way. It was done in the strength of his life.

God did him a favor and chased him out into the desert for forty years. Finally the call came again. The first time his response had possibly been, "Nobody could be any more ready or qualified than I am." But this time he said, "Not me, Lord. I just haven't got it." The Lord said, "I know that, Moses. I've just been waiting for you to find it out. You don't have it, but I do. Go do the job in dependence upon Me." The upshot was that Moses got another stick, but this time all he did was wave it over the water and he got rid of the whole Egyptian army with one swing. You see, faith is expecting God to be and do something in a situation in which we know by experience that we cannot be and do what is required.

Let's see how this works by imagining a kind of day in which we really need to use faith in order to express the life and love of God. You may have had a day something like this yourself sometime. It begins as you wake up a half hour past the time the alarm you forgot to set was supposed to go off. You're late! You try to dress quickly while shouting downstairs to your wife that you won't have time for breakfast, just toast and coffee. Good thing, because your wife is not downstairs, she's still in bed. She struggles out to have the toast and coffee ready by the time you patch up that shaving nick on your chin. The toast is burned, but the coffee looks good. Oops! A little hot! You jump and the coffee spills all over your suit. Another ten minutes to change. Finally you get in the car and turn the key. Nothing. The battery is dead! But it's your neighbor's day off and in only twenty more minutes he gets your car going with his battery and you're off. Not far off, though. A couple of blocks away, someone else who got up late runs a stop sign and removes the right front fender of your new car. Now, that's what I call a bad day! It's also a wonderful opportunity to use faith!

If you respond to that situation with your human soul-life, it will be either on the basis of how you think about it (the mind) or how you feel about it (the emotions). Depending upon how you think about it and feel about it, you will make a choice (the will) to take appropriate action.

Right now, you don't feel very good about it. You're irritated beyond human endurance and you feel like giving the other driver a punch in the mouth, or at least telling him off in no uncertain terms. You get out of the car with your emotions in control.

Suddenly the thought strikes you that you are a Christian and that you're not supposed to act like this! Now you begin to switch from how you feel about it to how you think about it. Your mind sends the signal to your body, you grit your teeth, and the look on your face switches from anger to a slightly phony smile pasted on a still slightly reddened face. Somehow you manage to be polite, even kind, and afterward you pat yourself on the back a little for not having behaved like an unbeliever. Unfortunately, it's not true. You behaved exactly like an unbeliever, for it took no faith and it took no God to do what you did!

What's the alternative? Faith! It begins with recognizing that those feelings of anger, impatience, and frustration are simply symptoms, warning signals, that the flesh, not the Spirit, is in control. Jesus doesn't act that way, so it must be you acting independently from Him.

The next step is to confess that you don't have the goods, just like Moses. "Lord, you know how this day has gone and You know that I just don't have enough love to really respond to this situation and this man as Jesus would. In my flesh there dwells no good thing."

But the confession doesn't end there. "Lord, I know that You do love this man. You loved him so much that You died for him. And I know that You are not impatient and irritated and upset and vindictive. I know that You are love and peace and joy. Lord, I submit myself to You and ask You to be love and peace and joy in me. Jesus, live through me right now!"

That's faith, and because God responds to faith, He will immediately begin to sweep through your entire being and your submissive soul will actually begin to experience the love of God and the peace of the Spirit. Accordingly, you will behave differently with your body, but the source will be the Spirit, and the righteousness will be His, not yours. God will be glorified in your life, because it will not really be your life that is expressed, but something beyond you: the life of Jesus manifested in your mortal body!

This is the simple secret of living that I have been discovering recently! I have personally experienced God living in and through me in all kinds of situations. Loving the unlovely, regarding another brother more highly than myself, being patient with my wife and kids, overcoming a problem of lust, not coveting another's position or ability, and a host of other everyday things that I have simply found that I cannot do apart from the indwelling life of Jesus Christ! I don't mean to say that having discovered this my life is always perfect now. Not at all. There are many times when I forget and presumptuously take over in my human strength. And other times when the flesh gets control and I just don't want Christ to take over; times when I'd rather just be myself and fight back at the world. But those times are sin, no bones about it, and they have to be confessed and covered by His blood. But, by the grace of God, they are also becoming less frequent, as by experience I learn the tremendous potential which is mine for victory in Christ.

Abiding in Christ does not mean going around with Jesus on my mind all the time. Few minds are equipped to concentrate effectively on two things at once. But abiding in Christ does mean turning inwardly to Him in the spirit the moment I face a situation which tends to bring the flesh into action. The process I described in the illustration above sounds long and drawn-out on paper, but in life it can all take place in the flash of a second. And the more you learn to live by Christ, the more spontaneous it becomes. You'll soon begin to frequently experience Christ expressing His life through you without your having consciously to call upon Him. This happens as the soul learns its proper place of submission to the Spirit. But if you get to the point where you get presumptuous again, you'll quickly be reminded by your own failure that you need to exercise faith to live the abundant life!

Paul called this spontaneous Christ-life "the law of the Spirit of life in Christ Jesus" (Romans 6:2). And he said that it sets us free from "the law of sin and of death." These "laws" are not laws like the legislation enacted by the government. They are principles of order in the universe, like the law of gravity. In fact, the law of sin and death is sort of the spiritual equivalant of the law of gravity. It is always there, pulling us down, but it can be overcome, by the law of life.

Think of it like this: A rock is always controlled by the law of gravity because it is dead, without life. No matter how many times you drop it, it will always fall. But climb on your roof and drop a bird! Does he fall? Of course not. Why not? Because he has life, and as soon as he begins to express that life he overcomes the law of gravity. It's still there, but it can't control him.

The rock is like the old man. Without spiritual life, the law of sin and death always pulls him down. But the bird is like the new man. He has spiritual life, and if he will only use it, he will be an overcomer. God hasn't repealed the law of sin and death; He has just turned the rocks into birds! But suppose the bird doesn't express the life he has? He drops like a rock. That's why Christians, new men, sometimes act like the old man—they just don't express the life they have. Because they don't use faith!

The Bible says that faith comes by hearing (or otherwise being exposed to) the Word of God (Romans 10:17). Why? Because it is in the Word of God that we find the facts about spiritual things, about God, about ourselves. You can't just have faith in and of itself; you must have faith in something. Everyone does, as a matter of fact. The question is, What is your faith in? Yourself, or God? By discovering the revealed facts in the Word of God, you'll find where to place your faith, because you'll discover who is really trustworthy and faithful and able to perform in every situation. Exercising that faith, you'll prove God, and your faith will grow.

Another thing I have learned about this matter of Christ living in me is that it is certainly not an inactive life. I think a lot of people get the idea, when they hear someone say, "You can't do it—Christ has to do it," that the Christian life is just sitting in a rocking chair someplace while Jesus is out in the world "doing it." This is not at all true. God will work, but through you. He doesn't bypass you; He wants to use you. The soul and body are not eliminated; they are controlled by His Spirit in your spirit. The thing that is required is that they be submissive, not rebellious toward the Spirit. God wants you to place yourself in situations with complete confidence that He will work in and through you to accomplish His purpose.

Read the fourth chapter of Romans and you'll find that this is exactly what Abraham did. The Word stated that he was to become a father (Romans 4:17). By hearing the Word he got faith. He then took note of the situation (Romans 4:19) and found that in and of himself he was incapable of fulfilling God's purpose. So he confessed, "I can't, but You can, Lord." Growing strong in faith (Romans 4:20), he then placed himself in the situation by the obedience of faith. He went to Sarah as a husband to a wife, but his confidence was that God "was able. . .to perform" (Romans 4:21). And God did. The son of Abraham—but he is called the son of faith and God got the glory!

I said in the first chapter that "God is love and He wants the world to know it." You and I have been chosen to show to the world the love of God. But this can only happen as we learn to *love by faith.*

Here's how it works for me: First I have to learn to recognize the symptoms of the flesh in action as well as the situations which tend to arouse it to that action. Read Galatians 5:19-21 for a descriptive list. And don't get hung up on idolatry and sorcery. These may not be your problems, but how about anger, arguing, or jealousy? At any rate, whenever I find myself behaving in an unchristlike way, I must recognize that this is the flesh in action. Then I need to learn to let these things act as flashing red lights to my spirit. If you're driving and you see a flashing red light, what do you do? You slow down, and begin to figure out what action you need to take to avoid the danger that may be represented.

Spiritually, when I see one of these flashers, the action I must take is to confess that "I cannot, but You can, Lord." By doing this I bring my human life into submission to His own, and express faith that He will meet the need. Faith brings God into action, and the result is the exciting experience of my own attitudes, thoughts, and feelings being conformed and transformed to those of Jesus!

I have applied this especially to meeting the irritations of everyday life, since this is where most of us have our greatest problems. But it applies equally to every situation. We are to live by faith! As we gather for fellowship, we need to trust God to express Himself through us in love and ministry toward one another. As we pray for the sick, we need to trust Christ to perform that which He is able, and not to trust in our prayers or feelings about the matter. As we witness and share Christ with others, we must learn to do it with a quiet confidence that God is working by His Spirit, and that the results will not come from the persuasive words of man's wisdom. There is not a single area of your life where God does not want to be manifested, and where you do not need to submit your human life to Him and trust Him to be your life!

We had an exciting illustration of this during the time that this book was being written. A nurse whom I'll call Carol had committed her life to Christ a few months previously and was coming to our home once a week with a few other new Christians for Bible study and fellowship. Carol shared with us that she felt God was displeased with her smoking. It was something that controlled her, and she was beginning to become aware that Christians were to be controlled only by the Holy Spirit. She had been trying to quit, and had not smoked for several weeks, but it was a real moment-by-moment struggle. Then suddenly, during a phone conversation with a Christian friend, the simple truth suddenly struck her that Christ-in-her could do what she could not. The Holy Spirit had shown her that Christ is stronger than her habit, and all she really had to do was trust Him instead of fighting it herself. She did, and has been experiencing a whole new kind of victory in her life. But even beyond that, as she was sharing this with us, she looked up with a surprised look on her face and said, "You know, I think I could trust Christ for His love and His courage, just like I've trusted Him for strength in this!" I know this is going to be a big breakthrough for Carol, for at home she faces an alcoholic husband and an unbelieving family.

This secret, this mystery of godliness, is something that has to be revealed by the Spirit. We had shared these things with Carol and the others many times, but now it is real for her. In this last couple of years the sixth chapter of Romans has become one of my favorite and most helpful passages of Scripture. But so many Christians tell me, "It's too hard to understand. I just can't get it." It's really not difficult at all once the Spirit makes it real to you. The discovery that Carol made is really summed up in these verses:

Therefore do not let sin reign in your mortal body that you should obey its lusts, and do not go on presenting the members of your body to sin as instruments of unrighteousness; but present yourselves to God as those alive from the dead, and your members as instruments of righteousness to God. For sin shall not be master over you (Romans 6:12-14).

What is Paul saying here? Simply that as the old man, you had no option but to present "the members of your body to sin." That is, without the presence of Christ in your life, the actions of your body were always independent from God and sin was your master. Now, as the new man, you have another option: Now you can "present yourselves to God." How do you do that? By that simple affirmation of faith, "I can't, Lord, but You can. You're within me and I submit to You and trust you." We present ourselves to sin by simply refusing or ignoring the option of presenting ourselves to God. But present yourself to God, by means of an act of the obedience of faith, and the result is that "sin shall not be master over You." The two primary lessons we have to learn are, one, that it really is possible to let the Spirit within control us and be our life; and, two, to remember to turn to Christ in our spirit when we are confronted with that situation which we cannot control or conquer in our own human lives.

This is what Paul means when he talks about the mind that is set on the Spirit (Romans 8:5-8). He says it is life and peace! Why? Because the mind that is turned toward the Spirit in the confidence of faith is the mind that is open and available to the supply of all that the Spirit of God is—life and peace and joy and love and victory! In contrast, the mind set on the flesh is death, the constant bone-grinding frustration of Romans 7, always trying, and always failing.

Paul goes so far as to say that the requirement of the law is fulfilled in us who walk not after the flesh, but after the Spirit (Romans 8:4). Do you want to really be able to live up to the Ten Commandments? This is the way. "Those who are in the flesh cannot please God" (Romans 8:8), but by inference, those who are in the Spirit can please God! Think of it: Your life pleasing God. That really makes life worth living!

The Christian life is Christ! The mystery of godliness is Christ in you! The key is the "obedience of faith" (Romans 1:5; 16:26). Never forget that God's primary purpose for you in this world is to be an expression of His own nature. He wants you to be a continual manifestation of the life of Jesus. And though there are ten thousand ways that this life can and will be expressed, essentially it looks like love! You are a new man. There is no reason in the world why you cannot be victorious and triumphant by the law of the Spirit of life in Christ Jesus if you want to and if you will! Everything else is peripheral compared to this. If we do this, the rest will follow.

"For whatever is born of God overcomes the world; and this is the victory that has overcome the world—our faith" (1 John 5:4).

10

YOU, IN THE MINISTRY

His intention was the perfecting and the full equipping of the saints (His consecrated people) [that they should do] the work of ministering toward building up Christ's body (the church) (Ephesians 4:12, Amplified Bible).

Let's recap briefly. So far, I've said that God's basic purpose in creating us was that we might be expressions of Him in this world; that He uniquely created us body, soul, and spirit so that we can contain His own Spirit life within us; that as we turn to Him He wonderfully equips us by indwelling and clothing us with His Spirit; and that He has provided that by the means of the obedience of faith we can actually be everyday spontaneous expressions of the life and love of God.

I've said all of that to say this: The spontaneous expression of the life of God in each individual believer is what the New Testament calls "the ministry." In other words, every person who has Christ dwelling in him is a Christian and every Christian is in "the ministry" because the ministry is simply the manifestation of the Spirit of God in you! You—yes, you—are in the ministry! And just as much so as any one else in the world! (See chapter 16 for an explanation of special workers, i.e., appostles, etc., and their ministries.)

I don't want to seem negative about anyone or anything, but it is simply impossible at this point not to mention the immense contrast between this statement and the generally accepted concept of the ministry both in our society and in the overwhelming majority of the professing Christian churches. In our day, it is almost impossible for anyone to think of Christianity without thinking of a special class of Christians recognized as clergymen or as the ministers of the church. A great many people regard the clergy as being the more spiritual class of Christians, and almost everyone accepts without challenge the idea that they are more qualified, perhaps even the only ones qualified, to minister. Among the professing Christian churches, there is probably not a single doctrine more universally held than the doctrine of a clergy class of ministers, and it is completely contrary to the basic doctrine of the church in the New Testament!

The New Testament teaching is that the church is a body in which every member has a necessary function, a ministry, toward the rest of the body and that each ministry is equally as important as any other (1 Corinthians 12:7-27). This ministry of the body was taught and practiced, and never even questioned until near the close of the first century. It was at this time that the deeds, and soon after the doctrine of the Nicolaitans arose (Revelation 2:6,15). Nicolaitan means "conqueror of the laity." It evidently began with a few who through ability, personality, ambition, or desire for power began to be predominant in the local churches. Some of them were probably thrust into these responsibilities by the apathy of their fellow Christians who remained silent and failed to exercise the ministries God had given them. The centralized ministry of the few to the many came to be called the "deeds of the Nicolaitans." To support their activity there soon arose the "doctrine of the Nicolaitans," and the division that Paul so vigorously opposed was introduced into the body of Christ (1 Corinthians 12:22-25). This was not a division into separate sects with varying doctrines; this was the division of each local assembly into two classes of Christians, the ministers and the laymen.

After the Reformation, the priesthood of the believers (1 Peter 2:5,9) was stoutly preached, but to many it only meant that individual Christians could now confess directly to God, and the concept of a clergy class was continued in the church. But the reformation is not yet completed, because the bride is not yet ready for her bridegroom, and one of the most basic truths that the Holy Spirit is restoring to the church today is the truth of the ministry of all of God's people in the body. And this is what lies at the heart of the small-group movement today—the effort to get God's people into an atmosphere where they can share what God has given them—the return of the ministry to God's people!

I don't think that the average evangelical clergyman is doing what he is doing out of a false motivation. Not at all. Many are doing the best job that can be done within the light that most of us have been walking in for so long. It's just that as God shows the church more of His wonderful calling and purpose, we want to be quick to adjust, to broaden the scope of the ministry to *all* who have the same Holy Spirit and holy desire to minister the things of Christ.

For several years, I spent quite a bit of time speaking to various congregations within the institutional church. Much of the time, I challenged the people to greater involvement and committment. Almost always, after such a meeting, I would be approached by some young man who, with shining face, would share with me that he was planning to make the big step—he was going into the ministry. This usually represented a very real step of commitment and sacrifice to him, and frequently sprang out of an inner compulsion to give out what God had put within him. Even though I rejoiced at his desire to abandon all to serve God, there was always a feeling of sadness that swept over me as well. Why was it not possible for him to be "in the ministry" right in his local church? Why, for everyone like him, would I also meet a dozen others who, with looks of defeat and resignation, would share with me that they would like to do more, but after all they were "just laymen"? We have got to see that each believer is intended by God to have a ministry to his fellow believers, that the normal place of that ministry is within and to the local church, and that there is no such thing as a class of believers who are more or less qualified than another to carry out this ministry!

A professional football coach was once asked, "What contribution does professional football make toward physical fitness in our country?" His answer was, "Professional football makes no real contribution to physical fitness in this country. Professional football consists of 22 men down on the field who desperately need rest, and 100,000 people in the stands who desperately need exercise!" Unlike football, Christianity was never intended to become a spectator sport!

Part of the problem arises from a single scripture passage —Ephesians 4:11-12—and the King James translation of it.

> *And he gave some, apostles; and some, prophets; and some, evangelists; and some, pastors and teachers; for the perfecting of the saints, for the work of the ministry, for the edifying of the body of Christ.*

Later, we'll talk about just what each of these gifts mentioned in verse 11 is and does, but for now I want you to see the problem in verse 12. The way it is worded in the King James Version, it sounds as though these men in verse 11 are to do three things:

1. Perfect the saints
2. Do the work of the ministry
3. Edify the body of Christ

The truth of the matter, however, is that the early Greek texts of this verse do not call for the insertion of the commas in verse 12. In addition, the word translated "perfecting" really should be translated "equipping." With these necessary corrections, the passage tells us that God gave gifts:

> *To equip the saints to do the work of the minstry for the building up of the body of Christ.*

Who is to do the work of the ministry? The saints are to do the work of the ministry! What about the special education and preparation necessary to minister? You will never understand the church until you grasp fully the fact that the qualification for ministry in the church is never the development of the soul-life but the possession of the life of Jesus Christ in your spirit! The ministry is the manifestation of the life of Christ in you! And here I want to make one of the most important statements in this book: The local church of the Lord Jesus Christ in its simplest and purest form is simply a group of Christians gathered together to let the life of Jesus be expressed in them toward one another.

I have often seen new Christians who probably didn't know a single verse of Scripture have a wonderful ministry in the lives of others. I know one brother who never seems to say anything very bright in ordinary conversation, but through whom God manifests Himself in an unusual way through the gift of prophecy. In some gatherings I have been in, it is not at all unusual to have children minister something God has given them. Ministry is simply that principle of the treasure in earthen vessels in action (2 Corinthians 4:7). To bring glory to Himself, God uses the simple and humble to bring down the wisdom of the mighty. And if He is going to be glorified, that which comes forth in ministry must have Him as the source.

In the last chapter, I mentioned that the expressed life of Jesus looks like love. This is because God is love and the expression of His life is always true to His nature (1 John 4:8-16). So ministry, in essence, is simply the flow of the love of God through you.

But love, like faith, must have an object. You can't just stand in a vacuum and love; you must love someone or something. God wants you to have a real ministry, and that ministry will be a ministry of love with someone as the object. The type of ministry it is will depend upon who the object is. Basically there are three objects of the love of God flowing through you. Every Christian is involved in these three basic types of ministry simply because Christ dwells in him.

MINISTRY TO GOD

The first and foremost direction for the flow of the love of God in you is upward. This is ministry to God. Barnabas, Paul, and the others in the church at Antioch were "ministering to the Lord" when the Holy Spirit spoke to them (Acts 13:2). What does this mean? You and I think of the Lord ministering to us; but what of our ministry to Him? This ministry is worship, and it is simply the spontaneous expression of the Holy Spirit if we will yield to Him.

Look at it like this: If God is love, whom did He love before He created anything? Love must have an object; who was the object? It's not difficult to realize that before anything was created, there was an unceasing flow of love within the Godhead. Now that the Holy Spirit dwells in you and me, we're caught up in the crossfire of that love! Isn't that terrific? "We love, because He first loved us" (1 John 4:19). And that love toward God just springs up spontaneously from the spirit of the believer.

Recently a student shared with me an experience he had had. While visiting a friend, he had picked up a book on systematic theology which he described as "very dead and dry." But something in it caught his eye. There was a section on the Godhead that really clicked with his spirit. Suddenly, he said, "I just fell to my knees and began to worship and praise God. I just had to spend some time loving Him." This is the ministry of worship in spirit and in truth, and every Christian is qualified for it because Christ dwells in him.

MINISTRY TO UNBELIEVERS

Upward is not the only direction the love of God flows through you, however. It also wants to flow outward. God has a ministry for you in the lives of people. Some of these will be people who don't know Jesus Christ themselves. The ministry of the Spirit through you to them is called "the ministry of reconciliation," because the purpose is to reconcile, or bring them back, to God.

Therefore if any man is in Christ, he is a new creature; the old things passed away; behold, new things have come. Now all these things are from God, who reconciled us to Himself through Christ, and gave us the ministry of reconciliation, namely, that God was in Christ reconciling the world to Himself (2 Corinthians 5:17-19).

This is what we refer to as evangelism. The heart of it is God in a man, expressing His love to other men in order to win them to Himself. And it is part of the life of everyone who is "in Christ." God has also placed in the church certain ones as evangelists, but this does not change the principle that each believer is to be used as a channel for the love of God in word and deed toward people who are not Christians. God wants to use you to love someone into the kingdom of God!

Recently, I was with a group of Christians which included a man whom God has used in winning some of the top political figures in our country to Christ. He was asked how he does it: How can you win such highly placed and influential men? His answer: "I just love 'em!"

Later in this book, we'll talk more about evangelism as it is carried on by the evangelists and by the body of Christ as a whole. But for now, let's look at the third ministry that God wants you to have as a Christian.

MINISTRY TO BELIEVERS

As every man hath received the gift, even so minister the same one to another, as good stewards of the manifold grace of God (1 Peter 4:10, King James Version).

This is probably the most overlooked ministry of all. At least we hear the other two talked about from time to time, if not practiced. But the ministry which God intends each believer to have toward the rest of the local body of Christ is seldom even mentioned. Yet this ministry, the flow of the life and love of God through you toward other believers, is the heart and substance of the church. And wherever it is quenched or limited, the church has been, is now, and always will be weak, floundering, and ineffective to a large measure. God has a better thing in mind.

> *The whole body. . ., when each part [with power adapted to its need] is working properly (in all its functions), grows to full maturity, building itself up in love (Ephesians 4:16, Amplified Bible).*

The strong, mature church can only result from a full exercise of the ministries of everyone in it toward the rest of the church. Just as our human bodies need regular exercise to remain healthy, so does the body of Christ. If you were to keep a normally healthy arm immobile in a cast for two years, there would be little resemblance of a healthy arm when the cast was removed. It would be a lifeless stick, without strength, stiff and completely unresponsive to the signals sent it from the head of the body. Sound familiar? On the other hand, exercise that arm regularly, and no matter how weak it may be, if it has life it will daily increase in strength and ability.

Nearly everyone realizes that there is a great lack of spiritual maturity in the church today. But what to do about it? In the natural realm, maturity is largely a matter of learning to do things by yourself, for yourself, and for others. How do you learn to do this? By doing! By beginning to feed yourself, to tie your own shoes, to button your shirt. Of course it's awkward in the beginning, but it's necessary. How else would you learn?

So, in the church, believers must grow by learning gradually to exercise the gifts God has given them. If someone does everything for them, they will never learn. Each Christian must be in the position of having to depend upon the Lord for His leading, life, and power. And then he must be given the opportunity to share what God gives him, even if it is not all we might hope for in the beginning. Maturity is a process of growth, but it needs exercise as well as food to take place.

In the past couple of years I have seen some amazing growth among Christians involved in this kind of fellowship. I have come to the conclusion that this growth comes as a result of each one exercising spiritually in ministry to the rest and at the same time feeding one another with the fantastic diversity of spiritual diet that can only come from this broad-based ministry. The result: fruitfulness and maturity beyond the usual. One student within a few months of his conversion had rented an old house on the North Side of Chicago and was taking in hippies, seeing them saved and also delivered from drugs. I know a young married man who won both his brothers to the Lord in the first few months of his Christian life and now is conducting a weekly Bible study with his parents to win them. There is a seventeen-year-old boy who knows far more of the Word than most adults. And a housewife who has a Bible study each week in her home just for the other housewives whom she has won to the Lord in her one year as a Christian. And on and on it goes. Not instant maturity, but some wonderful growth. This is just what the Bible promises will result when believers begin to recognize the ministry that God has committed to them and begin to exercise it in fellowship with one another. For in each of these lives, the outward fruitfulness went hand in hand with their discovery that each of them had a ministry to the believers.

We need to see how very close this is to the heart of all that God desires to do. God's purpose for Adam was not to save him from sin and hell; he didn't even need that in the beginning. Nor was it to have fellowship with him or to have him raise a garden. God's purpose for Adam, and for every man, was that he might contain the life of God, live by the life of God, and express the life of God. And this is His purpose, His central desire and will for your life. You are a complete possibility for God. You are to have a ministry toward God and man that is solely dependent upon the Spirit of God within you and not on your own soulish capabilities.

And at the heart of this is the ministry of believers to one another when they are gathered for fellowship in the Spirit.

The experiential realization of your own personal ministry among the believers is so important to God's primary will for your life that you need to place it as a top priority. Anything in your own life or in the church that prevents or stifles this ministry of the saints is contrary to the basic will of God, no matter how worthwhile it may seem. On the other hand, as you discover your ministry, you will find the fulfillment that can only come from perfectly fitting into God's plan. One brother I know often says that if each Christian would only find his or her own place in the body of Christ and seek by the Spirit to express that ministry, the problems of the church would disappear overnight.

Few things have been as misrepresented as the church of Jesus Christ. We have seen it as a building of brick and mortar, as an institution, as a welfare committee, as a super-organization. No wonder our concept of the church is a cloudy one today. In reality, the church expressed locally is simply a group of people in whom Jesus dwells, gathering together to express the love of God in ministry to one another and to God, and then going out into the everyday world to do the same. You are the key! Christ dwells in you! In the church God recognizes no priesthood but that of all His people, no ministers but the saints, no ministry other than the expression of the Spirit of the living God in each Christian. God wants to give to you gifts of ministry which can be expressed in pure worship toward Him, in reconciling men to God, and in building up your fellow Christians!

The ministry is the life of God in you! This is the new wine of Jesus. But what of the wineskin? What can hold this new wine? What kind of church can provide the atmosphere for this kind of ministry? God has not left us without His provision here. In the next few chapters we're going to look at the wineskin designed by God, the living church of the New Testament!

11

A BODY FOR GOD

To Him be glory in the church and in Christ Jesus to all generation forever and ever. Amen (Ephesians 3:21).

It was a terrifying moment! I sat in my study suddenly realizing that I knew virtually nothing about the church. Yet I was being paid to be the leader of a local church and, ostensibly, to teach others about it. But at that moment I knew that I hadn't the faintest idea of what God's idea of the church really was! Not that I hadn't had some training, of course. I had taken courses on church organization and government, pastoral theology, Sunday school development, and so on. These courses had covered such topics as church membership, how to set up building-fund committees, how to select and appoint deacons, trustees, elders, and ushers, and, of course, how to conduct meetings. But after all that, I still didn't understand the church. In fact, it is astonishing how much misinformation I had picked up. For example, I have before me the syllabus from one of those courses which clearly states that "the pastor is the head of the church." Wow!

Then one day, in a local bookstore, I saw a book by Watchmen Nee—*The Normal Christian Church Life*—that looked interesting. I had read one or two of his books on Christian living and had been helped. I thought that this one would be much like the others, so I got it. A few days later, I sat down to read it. By the end of the introduction I was angry. But I couldn't put it down. By the eighth chapter I was worried, and by the last chapter I was frightened. What if he was right? Then I was dead wrong!

But after a day or two, I calmed down. After all, there were a lot more people who agreed with me than agreed with him. Besides, times have changed. This is another age. We just can't do things the same way today.

I put the book on the shelf and resolved never to be bothered with it again.

It wasn't going to be that easy. About that same time I had started reading the book of Acts in my devotions. I had read it many times before, of course. But this time I began to see things I hadn't noticed before. Time and time again passages leapt out at me and seemed to say "Nee was right, brother. You've missed the boat." For months I fought it, but there it was. The more I searched the Scriptures, the more I found how very different was the church of the New Testament from anything I knew or had even dreamed of. At the time I felt terribly threatened, but now I can see that the Holy Spirit was working to create within me a hunger to know what in the world God really wanted.

The thing that has impressed me the most from that time to this about the church of the first century was the amazing lack of institutionalism and the tremendous spontaneity behind what the people were and did. We need to remind ourselves that there were no churches before them, so they didn't inherit their ideas. They didn't have the New Testament yet. A few local groups had one or two letters from apostles, but not all did. Some of them had received personal teaching from the apostles, but not all had. The one thing they had in common, and this formed the heart of the apostles' teaching, was the life of Jesus Christ within them. They didn't know "how" to start or have a church. They only knew that Jesus was alive within them and that as they obeyed and lived by that life, certain things came naturally (or should I say, supernaturally?). The most obvious thing for them was to get together in their homes. And when they did, and the life of Christ was allowed to control them, they began to share Christ with one another as the Spirit led. I'm not even sure how much they realized it, but in doing this they were fulfilling the purpose of God. They were an expression of the life of God in the midst of a Satanically-controlled world system. They were lights in the darkness.

The burden of my heart in this book is to say that nothing has changed. God's purpose is still the same. And God's way of having a church is still the same. If there is to be an expression of the church as God wants it today, it will have to come as a result of believers getting together simply to live by His life. His life has not changed; it will produce the same fellowship that it produced in the first century, if it is simply allowed to do so. The only reason that we are even going to delve into the "form" of the church as seen in the New Testament is that this is a record of the working of His life in men. It will give you a measuring rod by which you can determine whether what you see and are is being produced by the same life. But nothing will be gained by adopting or imitating this or any other form. What God wants can only be produced by men who are possessed by His Spirit and expressing His life spontaneously.

The Bible describes the church as a living body. The purpose of your human body is to allow your invisible personality to respond to a physical, visible world and to be expressed in that same world. The purpose of Christ's body, the church, is much the same. The essence, or life, of the body is an invisible personality (Spirit), but the body makes expression of that life in the world possible. The problem of the body is the same problem you and I have individually: If it does not live by the Spirit within, it will express another life, its own. Because the body of Christ is made up of individuals, the most important thing we have to learn concerning the church is to live by the Spirit of Christ ourselves. Then, together, we will also express Him. The usual response of people who begin to see something of the New Testament pattern of the church is to try to "construct" a "New Testament church." I tried it myself, several times as a matter of fact. And it can't be done. You can't "construct" a church any more than you can "construct" a baby. A baby is formed by the imparting of life, by a birth. When a baby is born, it has a body with an outward physical appearance which can be seen and described. Its life causes that little body to perform certain functions that can be seen and described. But you cannot produce a life by constructing an imitation of the appearance and functions of that baby.

So it is with His church. Its outward appearance is seen in the New Testament. What you see is an accurate description. But we can't produce the life of God by simply reproducing the pattern of the church as seen in the New Testament. It must be born of God. And when it is, as it grows, it will take the right form as naturally as does a baby becoming a man. If you force it to take another form, because of ignorance or tradition, you'll pervert its growth, prevent its function, and limit its life. You just can't take Spirit-filled beings, teach them to behave as an institution, and expect them to grow in the Spirit. Yet I have seen it tried again and again in the name of the Lord.

The church is not only for Christ; it is of Christ. When God wanted a bride for Adam, He didn't create a new life. He took a part of Adam and made a bride for him. Her very essence, her life, was Adam. She was not for herself, she was for him. So, when God builds the church, the bride of Christ, He begins with Christ. Christ must be her essence, her life. And when He has finished, she will be given to Him as a bride. And no part of her will be man-made; she will be fashioned by God!

The Bible teaching of the church as the body of Christ is exciting to see in the spirit. We can't really see it otherwise, because our natural eyes see only individual people scattered all over the earth. But God sees all these people together as a whole. He says that we are "being built together into a dwelling of God in the Spirit" (Ephesians 2:22). Not just separate pieces, like a dismembered doll on a table, but "built together" into one thing, a body for God.

"That in Himself He might make the two into one new man, thus establishing peace, and might reconcile them both in one body to God" (Ephesians 2:15-16). In this verse Paul is speaking of the Jews who have come to Christ and the Gentiles who have done the same. In other words, all the Christians. And together we are "one body" and "one new man." Do you get the picture? God's ultimate purpose is not so much *men* expressing His life, but *a man* expressing His life. It's almost like—well, close your eyes and try to imagine the world with one giant of a man standing in the midst of it, towering over everyone. This is the way God sees His people: as one man, and that man is the body of Jesus Christ.

I know this is hard to understand, but in some places the identification of Christ and His body is so complete that the name of Christ is used where the writer obviously means the church. For instance, on the road to Damascus, Jesus said to Paul, "Why are you persecuting Me?" (Acts 9:4). But Paul was actually persecuting the church. And in 1 Corinthians 12:12, when Paul is describing the likeness of the human body to the church, he says "as the body is. . ., so also is Christ." What does all this mean? It means that if Christ is going to be expressed and known in the world today, it will be through the only body He has in the world, the church. The world will never know anything of Christ in our generation except as they see Him expressed through His body.

Jesus Christ has today almost no authority at all among the groups that call themselves by His name. The present position of Christ in the Gospel churches may be likened to that of a king in a limited, constitutional monarchy. He is lauded, feted and supported, but in every crisis someone else makes the decisions. Because of long and meticulous organization it is now possible for the youngest pastor just out of seminary to have more actual authority in a church than Jesus Christ has.[1]

What does it actually mean that Jesus is the head of the church? Obviously it's something that has to have a practical expression or it amounts to exactly nothing! Jesus is not interested in being the figurehead of a large and confused organization. Someone has said that if He is not lord of all, He is not lord at all.

As Dr. Tozer has suggested in the quote above, organization is a matter of mechanizing some function of the body so that it is no longer dependent upon a living contact with the head. A lady we know has had an electrical device placed within her body to regulate her heartbeat. Even if it receives no signal from her brain at all, her heart will go on beating precisely as it should. And this is just what organization does for the church. No, the church is meant to be an organism, not an organization.

In the human body, the brain exercises control by having a direct and immediate contact with each and every limb and organ. In the body of Christ, His headship is expressed by the Spirit of God influencing and directing all believers so that their thoughts, activities, and movements are coordinated without awkward organization and control by man. The reason so many groups become overly organized is either that they have lost this kind of sensitivity to the Spirit or they fear that they will lose it. The attempt to replace it with something else is sheer idolatry, and the result is that the body soon becomes a corpse.

The "organization" of a true expression of the body of Christ is simply love! I mean the kind of love we talked about in chapter 9, the love of God supplied through Jesus Christ to my soul. Paul says that this love "is the perfect bond of unity" (Colossians 3:14). So any other bond must be inferior to it. People begin to overorganize out of fear. They fear that certain situations or relationships will deteriorate if they do not insure them by organizing. "The one who fears is not perfected in love" (1 John 4:18).

Love, as we discovered much earlier, is a matter of life!

And the entire organization of the fellowship of believers is a matter of life. There must be an abundant, throbbing supply and flow of the life of Jesus in each believer or there cannot be a true expression of the church. As a matter of fact, one of the reasons we know so little about how the first-century church was set up is simply that much of it was never officially determined. And it was never intended to be. They were to live by the life, for this is the only thing that could fulfill God's purpose for their existence. If they could not do this there was certainly no reason for existing any other way. The life of the Lord Jesus, living in His body, is enough to cause that body to behave according to His nature. And that is all He wants!

I've often been asked if the New Testament church is practical for our day because of the fact that its seeming lack of organization makes it so vulnerable, so fragile, so instable. I agree that it is very fragile. But I think God wants it this way so that it's always dependent upon Him. In a highly organized church, if the life goes, there is still plenty of reason and ability to continue the operation. There is a building, a corporation, a salaried employee, committees, meetings, and so forth. It can die, but it cannot disappear. That's comparable to having someone die and not burying the corpse. God doesn't want corpses representing Him in this world. He'd rather have nothing at all. Yes, let's be so fragile that if the Spirit flees the scene, nothing will be left. Better that something once good, now turned bad, should disappear and God raise up something entirely new in its place. We don't have to organize to guarantee the on-going of the church. God has guaranteed that (Matthew 16:18). All we have to do is make sure that what we are *is* the church, a living body alive with His holy and divine life.

Holding fast to the Head, from whom the entire body, being supplied and held together by the joints and ligaments, grows with a growth which is from God (Colossians 2:19).

It's been surprising to me how, even after a group has learned something of what it means to gather as a body, we can so easily forget it. This has happened to our little group a couple of times. Usually it happens after we've had an unusually good meeting, one in which God has moved through various ones to meet others' needs in a wonderful way. Then we tend to get cocky. I'm not sure, but I think we feel subconsciously that it was something we did and not what He did. Or maybe, because God greatly used some particular kind of ministry in one gathering, someone will try to repeat it the next time with the hope that it will produce the same result.

I was once in a meeting where a brother was led to read one of the psalms while we were praying. There was nothing extraordinary about the way he read it, but the Spirit anointed it and the impact was amazing. The problem came when he decided to make this "his thing" and repeated it the next few weeks. The anointing had departed and it was death. Of course, we really know better than this, but the flesh takes over and we find ourselves in trouble if we are not careful to hold fast to the head. Some kinds of repetition may be fruitful, however. Few things are as effective in putting us in contact with the Head as having the body enter into praise and prayer and allowing Him to lead from there.

First Corinthians 12 is a wonderful revelation of the church as the body of Christ. It contains several principles of body-life which are important. The first of these concerns the matter of the practical expression of Jesus as head. Verse 18 says that "God has placed the members, each one of them, in the body, just as He desired." He knows so much better than we just what ministries will be needed, and He moves as the head to make sure that each ministry will be there when needed. I can remember that when I was pastoring in the institutional church, a small panic occurred when we lost our only organist. We frantically worried, Where can we go to get another organist? Oh, if we had only had sense enough to look to Jesus to see what He wanted us to do instead of all that singing. We might have seen a real work of God in our midst. Can you imagine the church in Ephesus begging the Corinthians to send them a prophet because they just lost the only one they had? Of course not. God will see that there is a prophet there when a prophet is really needed. Until then, we need not concern ourselves. God knows when there is going to be a need. And when the need arises, He will supply. "One and the same Spirit works all these things, distributing to each one individually just as He wills" (1 Corinthians 12:11). We need to have an absolute reliance upon Christ to either send someone into the body or to distribute a gift to someone already there when a ministry is required. This is one of the ways He controls the movements of the body as its head.

A second principle is that although the various parts of the body are very different, they are all part of the body. "All the members of the body, though they are many, are one body" (1 Corinthians 12:12). "And if they were all one member, where would the body be?" (1 Corinthians 12:19). Diversity is one of the most wonderful things about body ministry. I've often heard someone say that a certain clergyman is a wonderful teacher but not much of an evangelist. Or he is a good evangelist but a poor pastor. But in God's plan he is only supposed to be one part of the body. If he was part of a body-group, others would meet those other needs. A one-man ministry is one method that defeats God's goal of body-life. Another is the tendencey of people to fellowship according to their gift. One group emphasizes teaching, so it attracts those with that gift. Another group emphasizes healing, so it attracts people who are primarily interested in healing. As these groups become more and more sectarian, they will tend to try to make teachers or healers out of people who ought to be something else. Some groups place so much emphasis on evangelism that a brother with that gift is almost idolized, but one who speaks in tongues would be put out of the group. This kind of sectarianism is fatal to God's purpose for His body.

The third principle is that the function of every part is vitally important. The eye can not say to the hand, "I have no need of you" (1 Corinthians 12:21). It is also true that you, as an ear, cannot say, "Because I am not an eye, I am not a part of the body" (v. 16). In the flesh, there will always be those who will tend to dominate and those who are perfectly content to let them do so. But in the Spirit it's different. If you try to rationalize that you really have nothing worthwhile to contribute, you quench the Spirit and hurt both yourself and the body. True, at a particular meeting you may have nothing to share. But in the long haul, God has placed you in the body to minister, as He has anyone else. To hold back is a very serious matter. Someone may be in desperate need of something only you can give. You yourself desperately need the spiritual exercise of being used by the Spirit. Disobey the Spirit and you hurt God, others, and yourself.

On the other hand, if you are one who tends to be more aggressive by nature, you will have to recognize your tendency to dominate others and let the Spirit really give you grace to be silent much of the time when you may feel you have something very valuable to give. It could even be that God is giving the same prophecy, teaching, prayer, or whatever to more than one person in the group at the same time. The extroverts will have to learn to wait on the more reticent and to avoid running ahead of the Lord. To always speak out, to insist on the lead, to be impatient with the slower, quieter brother may be to totally undo what God desires to do in His body. There is more than one way of quenching the Spirit. A sign that God is really at work will be the spiritual discipline in a group that leads the naturally vocal to be more silent and the naturally quiet to greater confidence in God's ability to use them in ministry.

God even goes so far as to say that the parts of the body

which seem on the surface to have less value are actually the most important (1 Corinthians 12:22-24). Never despise someone's gift, not even your own. Don't gather with the saints just to receive, but to give as well. Be looking to Christ constantly to show you what part you are to be in His body. You are really important to what God wants.

A fourth important principle of body-life is that "we are members of one another" (Ephesians 4:25). I've already pointed out that the foundation of fellowship is love. Paul says, "The members should have the same care for one another. And if one member suffers, all the members suffer with it; if one member is honored, all the members rejoice with it" (1 Corinthians 12:25-26). This becomes really true when we live by His life. In His love, there is never any need for me to be jealous of your gift; when God uses you mightily, it's the same as if He were using me—I am a member of you! And if I get into a position spiritually where God can't use me, don't despise me; suffer, brother, suffer! Because we who are many are one body!

Wherever two parts come together in the human body there is a joint. When the parts move, there is friction in the joint. But the natural fluids of the body lubricate the joints to reduce the friction. In the body of Christ it is the same. And the lubrication that God supplies for the joints is the oil of the Spirit, the love of God. This is why Paul goes from chapter 12 to chapter 13 in 1 Corinthians. It is not (as some suppose) love instead of body-life or love instead of the gifts. Body-life with the gifts cannot function without a very generous dose of love. If there is one overall guiding principle for believers gathering together, it is "with humility of mind let each of you regard one another as more important than himself" (Philippians 2:3). And that is love!

The purpose of the body of Christ is to express something to the world that it can never know in any other way. That means it must be very different from the world. The world and the people in it are involved in a great struggle for survival. The survival of the fittest demands that each one cling to his own. But those in the body of Christ have all died. The struggle is over. They have nothing to fight for among themselves. They can lose everything and still possess everything. The opposite of the world is Christ. The opposite of take is give. The opposite of self is love.

As Christians we can't necessarily expect to show more intellectual cleverness, technical perfection, or organizational efficiency than the world can. But love, real divine love, is unknown in the world. So Jesus said, "By this all men will know that you are My disciples, if you have love for one another" (John 13:35). They may not like it; they may even hate it; but they are sure to recognize it! Love is the highest expression of divine life. As the manifestation of the person of the Lord Jesus Christ in His body, it is the most perfect reflection of God in the mirror of human existence. To live by His life and to love is what God wants from you and me!

Since that morning I described at the beginning of this chapter, I've spent quite a bit of time searching out the meaning of the church. I still feel like the most elementary beginner. The whole thing is so vast, so amazing. But this I know: God has a body on this earth and man can't start it or stop it. It's a work of the Spirit and man can't harness it, or organize it, or institutionalize it for his own ends. The Spirit will always slip through his fingers like little drops of mercury and come together again another place with another people. And when He does, it will always look the same again. It will look like the simple, primitive church of the New Testament, because it lives by and is formed by the same life. And that life is love!

In the rest of this book we're going to look in some detail at some of the more apparent outward aspects of the church. As I said, it is a body and it can be seen and described. But please don't try to imitate its form. Seek after its life and you will know God!

Now to Him who is able to do exceeding abundantly beyond all that we ask or think, according to the power that works within, to Him be the glory in the church and in Christ Jesus to all generations forever and ever. Amen (Ephesians 3:20-21).

I therefore, the prisoner of the Lord, entreat you to walk in a manner worthy of the calling with which you have been called, with all humility and gentleness, with patience, showing forbearance to one another in love, being diligent to preserve the unity of the Spirit in the bond of peace. There is one body and one Spirit (Ephesians 4:1-4).

12

THE CHURCH GATHERED

Let us consider how to stimulate one another to love and good deeds, not forsaking our own assembling together, as is the habit of some, but encouraging one another; and all the more, as you see the day drawing near (Hebrews 10:24-25).

The gatherings of the church are extremely simple but supremely important. Important, because the church gathered together furnishes one of the most beautiful and complete examples of the life of God expressed in this world. One brother, after seeing body-life functioning for the first time, said, "Wow! It's too bad we can't get this on television so the world could find out what the church really is." Well, I have some doubts about his plan, but I know what he feels. To see a group of Christians gathered together in a way that proclaims Christ as head of the church and lord of their lives is a wondrous thing, especially if you've never seen it before.

I also said these gatherings are simple. Simplicity is the key, as a matter of fact. Can you imagine anything more simple than a few believers sitting around someone's living room, sharing Christ with one another? And almost anything that distracts from that simplicity will usually be found to be soulish in origin and contrary to the purpose of God. Much prayerful care is needed to keep these simple gatherings from being perverted after the nature of organized religion. This is especially true if the believers involved have a background in the organized church. But even apart from that, man's soulish tendency to organize according to some system, and his spiritual laziness which leads him to follow a habit or tradition rather than seeking to be led of the Spirit will always tend to the same problem. The biggest part of the solution is to be aware of the potential problem and be looking to the Lord for His constant leading. That's why so much time was spent on the difference between soul and spirit earlier in the book. The gathering of the church is where it really shows!

One of the very first difficulties lies in the basic concept most of us have about "meetings." Recently, we had a young person fellowship with us for the first time. We were sitting around chatting in twos and threes. The conversation died down for a moment, and he suddenly looked up and said, "How do you go about starting this service?" Amused, we tried to share with him that we had not gathered to have a "service" or a "meeting." That's why I haven't used the word *meeting* in connection with this chapter. You may think that's just hairsplitting, but I believe some have a concept which carries with it the idea of a chairman who convenes and adjourns a meeting during which all business which is really meaningful is conducted, and apart from which nothing takes place that is really important. To have real fellowship in the Spirit, we need to get as far from that concept as we can.

Jesus said that if two or three of us get together in His name, that is all that is required (Matthew 18:20). He will be there too. And with you and me and Jesus there, the things we do can't be divided into secular and religious categories. But I've seen this happen so often, even in house-churches. As folks begin to come in, everyone chats freely and openly, sharing with one another whatever is on his heart. Then suddenly, when everyone has arrived, or when the designated time for the "meeting" has come, a deadly silence falls over the group. Everyone is aware of being in a "meeting" and begins to wonder when they should "contribute" their part. We have to avoid this, although probably every group will experience it from time to time.

Don't try to solve it with a soulish solution, however. In one group I visited they were always trying to get everyone there "on time." Those who didn't arrive by then were subtly accused of not having enough love for the others. Many other groups have tried to solve it by using music to artificially and emotionally create a "beginning" that is not from the Spirit.

The best thing is to simply be real and honest with one another. If one brother honestly feels that he should lead out in prayer, let him do it—but not just as an artificial means to convene the meeting. At other times there may be a period of silence as you wait on the Lord for direction. On the other hand, there will be many times when there is a real need for conversation in groups of two or three around the room. This may spontaneously lead to someone sharing something with the whole group, but either can be equally the work of the Spirit. By conversation, of course, I don't mean the silly, frivolous kind of talk which quenches the Spirit and which is condemned by Scripture. Nor do I mean to infer that prayer is not a valid way of beginning. In fact, there will be many times when the church will need to spend much time in deep prayer and praise to God before any ministry or sharing begins.

Another potentially very serious problem is that of replacing the leadership of the Spirit with either a human leader or with a predetermined form. As I mentioned, man is inherently lazy spiritually. Also, by long habit, he has trained his soul to recognize and respond to outer stimuli much more readily than it responds to the inner voice of the Spirit. This is why it becomes so very easy to drift into the habit of following a human leader rather than seeking to be led by God. Remaining sensitive to the Spirit requires spiritual discipline. There must be no unconfessed sin in your life, you must be in regular fellowship with God through prayer and His Word, you must be walking faithfully in all the light you have. On the other hand, all that is required to follow a leader or a form is to keep your eyes and ears open and not fall asleep. There have always been plenty of Christians who have been willing to take this easy way, with the result that Christ has not been allowed to be head of His own church and many have been led off into something other than what God really wanted in the situation.

Sometimes this problem is caused by someone who has a carnal desire to be in charge and to control others. This is usually rather easy to spot, even though it may look very spiritual on the surface. But a much more subtle form of this problem occurs when little by little the members of a fellowship group discover that one of their fellow members is a little more "spiritual" than the rest and can usually be relied upon to be walking in the Spirit. Then they begin to relax and subtly look to him for direction, imitating his actions or following his moods, rather than individually looking to the Spirit.

The basic tendency of the spirit of Antichrist is to elevate a man to replace God. This will eventually take a final world-dictator form, but in the meantime the spirit of Antichrist is already at work seeking to put men in the place of God in the church. (Antichrist means "instead of Christ" as well as "opposing Christ.") The people of God need to be very aware of this form of the enemy's deceit and resist his gaining control of the fellowship of the saints in this subtle way.

The key is to be always aware of being part of the body and responsive to the head. Then He will lead in all our activities together and we will be edified. As we learn to live by the Spirit of Christ moment by moment in our daily lives, the gatherings of the believers will be a delightfully spontaneous occurrence which will meet everyone's needs.

THE SETTING

I don't know why I missed this for so long, but a simple

study of the Acts and the epistles shows that the primary place used by the believers for regular gatherings was the private home. I believe there was good reason for this—good enough reason, as a matter of fact, to regard it as a pattern which is both workable and scriptural for today, breathed out by God to His apostles as part of His plan for the entire age of the church.

One of the most immediate and spontaneous results of the outpouring of the Spirit on the day of Pentecost was the constant fellowship which took place as the believers gathered in various homes to eat together (Acts 2:46). Of course, they used the temple (Acts 3:1) and, later, the synagogues (Acts 13:5;17:1-2) for public testimony and evangelism, but the primary fellowship of the saints was in their own homes. This continued throughout the following years. "Over twenty times we read of them carrying out their united worship in the home of a believer. Four times (Romans 16:5; 1 Corinthians 16:19; Colossians 4:15; Philemon 2) "the church in the house" is specifically mentioned.[2] Standard practice all through the New Testament was to gather in the informal family atmosphere of someone's house.

Remember that the Christians of that first century were either converted pagans or Jews. Most of the pagan religions of that time had the custom of building huge, ornate temples of worship. And the Jews had centered their religion around a certain building in a certain place for centuries. Even when scattered, the first thing they did was build a synagogue. So all of these new Christians had a strong natural tendency to build something special for religious purposes. Yet indications are that for the first two or three hundred years they built no special buildings for the purpose of worshiping Jesus Christ. Doesn't that tell you something? Oh, I know that some people say it was because they were always persecuted. But the fact is that there were periods of time when the church was not persecuted at all, but enjoyed great peace (Acts 9:31); even then there were no building committees.

There are some definite advantages to following God's plan in this matter. A recent report from United Press International estimated the real estate belonging to the professing church in the United States at $102 billion. Someone said that if this could all be turned into cash, we could give every refugee in the world a gift of $1,000. I don't know if this is accurate, but certainly a lot could be done for the poor and for the Lord's work in outreach. Also, this "edifice complex" can easily lead to pride based on values which are totally contrary to spiritual things (James 2:1-10), and necessitates organization which can become a problem for many of the reasons mentioned in the last chapter. Remember too that in Communist countries one of the first attacks on the church comes as the government appropriates church buildings, leaving God's people cut off from much of what they identified as church.

But there are indications that even in Communist China today there are hundreds of little house-churches still gathering. Many of these are the result of the ministry of Watchman Nee and others who planted this kind of church long before the Communists made it a necessity.

Taxation of church property is a much discussed topic here today. Could it be that God might be preparing His people in this country now for something like this in the future?

On the other hand, the church-in-the-home can be effective under many conditions where traditional buildings prove impossible. Under persecution, in high-rise city apartments, in rural communities where there are not enough Christians to support a building, in the jungles of Asia, or in the ghettos of America, people nearly always have one thing in common: some kind of home where a few others can come together for fellowship and ministry.

The informality of the home encourages spontaneous participation and the family nature of the local church. We've found a wonderful release just in the fact that we don't have to get all dressed up in our Sunday-go-to-meetin' clothes. This encourages many who can't afford to dress up. We've also found that the regular gathering of God's people in a home can be a great blessing to the host family.

But perhaps one of the greatest advantages to meeting in homes is that it keeps the group small. In a small group, relationships are more real and vital, and everyone is more likely to share. Gathering three hundred people together and giving everyone an opportunity to share would take an awfully long time, and almost certainly rule out those with less confidence in their ministry. God's people are a family and we ought to gather to love and share as a family. When the church grows too large for one home, let's meet in two homes, and then four, and then eight. Growing by dividing will spread the church out over a much greater area, influencing many more neighborhoods with the gospel. And from time to time, all the believers in the area can come together for united fellowship in a rented facility, such as an American Legion hall, which is available in just about every town and city, or even in the open air, weather permitting.

Let me add a couple of warnings here. As the local church grows, be sure to *stay* in homes. It's very easy to begin to rationalize away the principle when the time actually comes for expansion. Also, the division of God's people should never be on the basis of doctrine, race, economics, or natural compatibility. The best way to relocate as more than one group is to divide on the basis of where you live, Christians in each neighborhood getting together with those closest to them. By the way, even while only one home is necessary to accomodate a group, it may help to rotate the meeting place from one home to another occasionally. This will keep the group from becoming centered on any one host or home to the point where the church becomes known as "John Smith's group."

The most important thing about the setting in which the church gathers is that it be an atmosphere of love and informality, and that it be without preconceived ideas or arrangements regarding what will take place. The saints must be "at home" with one another and the Lord must be in charge, or there is very little reason for gathering. When you first begin, this won't come easily, but a little time, the casual atmosphere of a home, and much prayer will soon lead to the spontaneity the Lord desires.

"WHEN YOU ASSEMBLE"

So when we do come together, what should we do? Nobody can really tell you that but the Lord. But we can look at some of the things which will occur from time to time as Christians fellowship. One of the verses that most concisely describes a New Testament church session is 1 Corinthians 14:26:

> *What is the outcome then, brethren? When you assemble, each one has a psalm, has a teaching, has a revelation, has a tongue, has an interpretation. Let all things be done for edification.*

This is the heart of it. The only thing missing in this verse is that it couldn't be long enough to describe the vast variety possible, so the apostle just lists a few examples. Fellowship is the whole principle of the church-as-a-body put into action. Each person comes with a sense of looking to the Lord and an expectation of being used by Him to minister to the others according to His leading and their ministry gifts. There's no format, no program; just a principle that everything should be helpful to someone. And every verse in the New Testament which refers to the fellowship of the church describes the same kind of ministry.

Even the passage at the heading of this chapter—Hebrews 10:24-25—which is so often quoted to encourage people to go to church, mentions this mutual ministry. Why is it that God is so concerned that we not forsake the assembling of ourselves together? Is it just because He likes a crowd? He could gather people for a football game if that were it.

No, it's because something happens when believers come together this way that makes them all stronger and more like Jesus because of their continuing experience with the Spirit of God as they "stimulate one another."

I'm going to list several of the things which the Bible indicates will at various times be part of Christian fellowship. But don't get the idea that this list suggests any order of importance or arrangement. All of these things could occur in any one gathering, or any one activity could dominate an entire session in itself. We have had times when the Lord seemed to lead us to do nothing but pray the entire time we were together. Other times prayer has played a rather small part compared to other areas the Lord led us into. Also remember that in mentioning these things, we're not trying to achieve any kind of technical perfection, but to share some Scripture guidelines along which the Spirit will move from time to time.

Sharing experiences is a very basic part of fellowship. Remember that the local church is made up of some of the most exciting people in the world. God is at work in their lives every day. What better way to "stimulate" and "encourage one another" than to share what the Lord has done while we were apart. Many times the report of a definite answer to group prayer has become the occasion for a wonderful time of praise and worship. Of course, this shouldn't ever take the form of "reporting in" or any other forced kind of testimony meeting, but it is a tremendous thing to share the fresh experiences we have had with God in daily life. This could be an answer to prayer, a personal discovery in the Scriptures, a soul won to the Lord, or a thousand other things. If God is in it, He should be praised through sharing.

Of course, there is another kind of sharing that is equally important. That is the sharing of our defeats and failures. I think one of the toughest yet most valuable lessons the Lord can teach us is to be really open and honest with one another. Many of us feel that others will not accept us if we don't appear spiritual at all times. So we wear a mask. But if anything is basic to Christianity, it is honesty. The last place we should have to pretend is among the believers. If we're not loved and accepted there, we never will be anywhere. Some of our best sessions have come as someone just let down his hair and shared his problems. It happened to me while writing and rewriting the first few chapters of this book. It was slow going. The devil was really after me. One week I really became discouraged and down. On Sunday I finally was able to share reluctantly with the others what I was going through. The response was wonderful. They gathered around me, rebuked the devil, prayed for me, loved me, and promised to support me daily in prayer until the book was finished. What a change it made for me!

Still another kind of sharing is mentioned by James: "Confess your sins to one another, and pray for one another" (James 5:16). Of course, not all such things should be brought up in the larger gatherings. It might be wiser to share some just with the elders. But still there is room for some real openness in this area with one another. In the beginning when we first started to gather, we seemed to bog down for a while. Then one person finally broke down and admitted that he had a real problem accepting one of the others because of some things which had occurred in the past. This simple confession brought about a real healing of the situation, and helped some others who were having similar problems. I mark this as the real spiritual birth of our little fellowship group.

Prayer is another activity which forms a big part of fellowship. Sometimes it follows closely on the heels of sharing, as sharing often prompts either praise or intercession for another's needs. Prayer is a very big subject and it is impossible to even begin to treat it here, but there are a few things I want to say about it in direct connection with fellowship gatherings.

We need to remember that public prayer, like the sharing

of experiences or any other body ministry, must be done under the leading of the Spirit. Prayer is not a stop-gap measure. Done hypocritically, it will quench the Spirit as fast as anything can. Done in the Spirit, it is one of the most powerful weapons of spiritual warfare available to the body of Christ.

Something else to remember is the different forms that prayer can take. Prayer is not always an extended conversation by one person with God. Much of the prayer we have experienced sounds something like group conversation. One begins to pray and prays a few sentences, perhaps just on one thought. Another might pick it up and pray along the same line, and the next might change the subject. This eliminates the need for lists of prayer requests and allows the Spirit to lead various ones to pray about the same things. Again, informality is the key. Prayer should be simple enough that the inexperienced new convert feels free to join in without concern about how he sounds. One man who had never been able to pray publicly recently started fellowshiping with us, and it was a real milestone in his life when he prayed aloud in the group for the first time.

There should no more be a set time for prayer than for any other ministry in the body. We might go to prayer a dozen different times or we might pray once and that's it. During a time of sharing, for instance, it's not necessary to wait until we have finished sharing to go to prayer. Something one person shares might prompt another to pray about the matter shared, then another would go on sharing. Also, many problems can be taken care of if a few members of the body will only begin to pray silently when something out of order is going on. The Spirit will often move in and correct the problem without any public correction necessary.

Another aspect of prayer that is often overlooked is audible praise of God. "Let us continually offer up a sacrifice of praise to God, that is, the fruit of lips that give thanks to His name" (Hebrews 13:15). Many times, we're inclined to think only of singing as a means of praising God. This is good, but sometimes there is the limitation of always using another's words. God's people need to learn to speak the praises of God to Him, for this is a sacrifice that pleases Him. In the Old Testament, the praises of God were often spoken rather than sung. "And all the people shouted with a great shout when they praised Jehovah. . . ." Again and again the psalms ring out with the admonition to praise the Lord. How much more should we praise Him today now that His glory has been revealed in His Son and His Spirit poured out upon all flesh!

Singing is mentioned several times in the Bible as a function of believers gathered together (Matthew 26:30; Ephesians 5:19; Colossians 3:16). But it is an area where we really need to get rid of any institutional hangups some of us may have, and where we need to be aware of the fleshly tendencies as well.

Singing in unison, of course, is one very basic way of worshiping God. Some songs are full of praise to God. Others take the form of prayers of petition. Here we need to make sure that we really mean the words we are singing.

Worshiping God and praying to Him are not the only functions of singing, however. Paul speaks of "teaching and admonishing one another with psalms and hymns and spiritual songs" (Colossians 3:16). Whether we know it or not, we may derive a good deal of our understanding about God and His ways from the songs we sing. For this reason, again, we need to be aware of words. Many songs have been written to express someone's sentimental feelings about God, but the words may be actually contrary to Scripture. By singing these songs we may be teaching one another, and even ourselves, false ideas about God. Recently, however, I have heard several songs which are simply passages of Scripture set to music. It seems to me that we can't go very wrong singing Scripture to one another, and praising the Lord with Spirit-inspired psalms.

There can be much wonderful ministry in singing. I know of one woman who is frequently given songs by God. She sings them for those in her fellowship, and this is a source of great blessing. There are times when a particular song expresses the response of the entire body to the love of God more fully than anything else can. And as we sing scriptural songs, young believers and children will learn truths about God quickly.

One thing we need to be aware of is that singing within the fellowship of the body is not an artistic performance. If one person feels led by the Spirit to sing a song, let him sing. If others are led to join in, that's fine; if not, let him minister to them with his song. I'll never forget the first time I heard someone sing a solo in this kind of fellowship. I was shocked because she had not been asked. It seemed so presumptious. Then I realized how much of the old form I still had in me. God has asked her to sing. Was anything else necessary? Also it didn't matter if she was artistically up to par or not. She was not giving a concert; she was sharing her heart with her brothers and sisters in the Lord.

We do need to remember, however, that singing has a powerful affect upon the emotions. It is very easy to use it as a substitute for the Spirit. I once took a course in song-leading. We were taught that one of the chief duties of a song leader was to bring the people into a unity so they would be prepared to receive the preaching, and to use special invitational songs to influence people to commit their lives to Christ after the preaching. Singing in unison is able to create a false sense of unity and of belonging to one another that does not have to have any spiritual reality behind it. As such, it's often used even in political rallies and community sings. Praise God for fellowship in which the Spirit is our "song leader" and in which the singing is the result of unity, not the cause of it.

I don't know of any scriptural precedent as to what type of music can be used. I have fellowshiped in groups where they sang mostly hymns from a hymnbook, groups that sang mostly gospel choruses, and some that are developing a whole new kind of Christian music which has a distinct folk-music sound. These variations spring mostly from cultural backgrounds. It's of little importance whether someone plays the piano or the tambourine, so long as it springs from life and is a true expression of the Spirit of God in that person. If we are careful to let the Spirit lead and control in this area as in all other areas of ministry, He will lead us into some wonderful times of worship, praise, prayer, and ministry through singing.

There is one other type of singing that the Spirit may lead us into from time to time. Paul calls it "singing with the Spirit." This is not to say that any other singing we do should not also be with the Spirit, but the context of this passage in 1 Corinthians 14 shows that Paul is referring here to singing in other tongues. This is a ministry of the Spirit directly to God in which the Spirit supplies both the unknown language and the tune. Again, it may be a ministry of one individual or the entire group. When it's a group, it's a wonderful thing to see the harmony created by the Spirit without the group having any preconceived idea of a tune. I have witnessed this a few times. It sounded like the voices of angels giving praise to God on His throne. Of course, this kind of ministry should not take place where it would confuse and stumble others, and some feel there should be an interpretation of the song afterward, though the interpretation need not be sung to a tune.

Remember that singing can be a wonderful expression of the praise and joy we feel within, as well as a powerful means of teaching one another. But it is not more a part of fellowship than any other ministry. We should never feel that we have to sing when we come together. I have seen gatherings where there was not a song sung, yet there was a real atmosphere of worship. And I have been in gatherings where the Spirit directed us to sing and sing—times when we did little else. God is a God of great variety, praise His name! "Be filled with the Spirit, speaking to one another in psalms and hymns and spiritual songs, singing and making melody with your heart to the Lord" (Ephesians 5:18-19).

Paul urged Timothy to give special attention to the *reading of the Scripture* in the churches (1 Timothy 4:13). This is just what it seems to be: the reading of some passage of Scripture without comment or explanation. I have been surprised sometimes how often this seems to occur under the leading of the Spirit in fellowship. And the Spirit is able to take that Word and make it real to someone in need. I recall one time when a girl was struggling with a decision and someone who didn't even know about it read a chapter from the Old Testament which told her just what she needed to know. Later she shared with us that she had no idea that God's Word gave such specific teaching in that area. Also remember that our faith is based on what God has said and the reading of it can serve to strengthen our faith, even though we are already familiar with the passage.

Teaching is a specific gift of the Spirit, and we'll discuss it in greater detail in chapter 13. But obviously it is a significant part of the fellowship of the church. One of the great joys of teaching in the atmosphere of the body-ministry is the informality. A teacher might take only three minutes one time to teach something. Another time he might take an hour if necessary. I have had many people ask me if teaching doesn't lose out in body ministry. I suppose they are thinking of the prominent part it plays in the institutional church. But the truth is that there is every bit as much opportunity to teach, while still allowing all the other ministries as well. If the Spirit leads, no ministry has less or more importance than it deserves.

Also, the informality of home gatherings produces a kind of teaching which allows for asking questions and discussion. At Troas, Paul spent the entire night discoursing with the Christians (Acts 20:7). And the custom of asking questions evidently was common (1 Corinthians 14:35). A teacher should never be in such a hurry that he leaves someone confused if a simple question or two will clarify it. I have seen occasions where one brother began to teach, someone asked a question, the teacher partly answered it and another teacher chimed in and finished it. One night four young men came to a gathering I was in, and we found that God had led each of them to prepare a teaching, all of them on the same subject. The first talked about ten minutes, the second took up where he left off, then the third, followed by the fourth. None of them had any idea what the others planned, yet the teaching all tied together as if they had collaborated.

All of the *gifts of the Spirit* will play a part in the ministry of Christians to one another from time to time. Since all of chapter 13 is devoted to the gifts, we won't go into them at length here. Just keep in mind that the body is made up of many members and that the Lord's way of supplying is to "distribute to each one individually as He wills." Many times the gift itself is not resident in an individual permanently, but is given to him for the body at the time it's needed. It's even possible that he would never manifest that particular gift again. So be aware that the Lord may use someone very unexpectedly to minister a gift. We need to be continually looking to Christ as the head of His body. All of these activities are prompted by the Spirit of God and can be expected whenever two or three gather in His name.

Sharing a meal was often a part of the fellowship of the early Christians (Acts 2:46). This fits in perfectly with the at-home family atmosphere of the children of God. We've found that sharing a simple potluck meal together on Sundays allows us to spend more time together. It's also a wonderful expression of the sharing nature of Christian fellowship. After the meal, as the ladies pick up (we use paper plates, etc.) the men can consider any decisions that relate to the church, and afterward fellowship has a chance to move spontaneously to more specific ministry. Or it might work out better to plan the meal at the conclusion of your time together.

The Lord's supper, the sharing of the bread and the cup which represent the body and the blood of the Lord, went hand-in-hand with this common meal in the New Testament. In fact, it sometimes became a problem when the two were confused (1 Corinthians 11:20-21). Though they are different, they can each be a vital part of fellowship. For a while, we were in the habit of sharing the Lord's Supper at the end of our time together. Then we discovered that sometimes someone had to leave earlier than expected, or that having a set way of ending created subtle pressures which were not healthy. Now we simply have the bread and cup sitting out in the room and at any time, as the Spirit leads, anyone of the brothers will bless it and begin to pass it around. The bread and cup are not only representative of the Lord's sacrifice for us, but of the unity of the body; occasionally if something has happened to disrupt that unity we don't break bread rather than pretend something that isn't there. But usually it is part of our gathering together. My wife and I sometimes share this symbolic meal when one or two Christians visit our home apart from the regular gatherings. Incidentally, some people ask about whether to use wine or unfermented grape juice. I can't see becoming legalistic about either. Personally I prefer using wine, since it's my understanding that this was used in New Testament times (1 Corinthians 11:21). Also, the wine serves as an antiseptic for the common cup.

All of these things put together make up the fellowship of the church of Jesus Christ. He is central, and His life is simply expressed in these various ways. I've avoided giving a lot of detail on most of these activities, because they are matters of life, not legislation. Each group and each believer must seek the guidance of the Spirit in the light of His Word. None of the things in this chapter has been intended as a rule or technique for body-ministry. But some of us have been so used to meeting an entirely different way, and it is good to see the almost endless variety that God has for us. I can't repeat too often that what is really required is that we live by His life, always looking to the Spirit in complete dependence, for "apart from Me you can do nothing" (John 15:5). Only as we live by His life within us can all of these things come into focus with His purpose. The church is a body, you are a member, and the Spirit of God wants to use you in edifying the other believers and in expressing His life and nature on earth. "If we walk in the light as He Himself is in the light, we have fellowship with one another" (1 John 1:7). Christ is building His church and as we abide in Him we're going to see some truly amazing and wonderful things before the Day of the Lord.

(For some, this chapter raises questions which I prefer to comment on elsewhere. See the Appendix for a question-answer discussion on women in the church, the training of children, weddings, and funerals.)

"FOR THE COMMON GOOD"

Now concerning spiritual gifts, brethren, I do not want you to be unaware (1 Corinthians 12:1).

To each one is given the manifestation of the Spirit for the common good (1 Corinthians 12:7).

Since we have gifts that differ according to the grace given to us, let each exercise them accordingly (Romans 12:6).

In his book, *Aglow with the Spirit* (p. 1), Robert Frost tells of a college student who once remarked, "To me, the Holy Spirit is nothing more than kind of a white oblong blur." I have noticed that many Christians, including some whose concept of the Holy Spirit is noticeably clearer than that student's, are still very hazy about the operation of the gifts of the Spirit. But it's really important to have a good understanding of these things if we are to see a local expression of the body of Christ functioning as it should. In fact, the lack or imbalance of the gifts of the Spirit is one of the major reasons that a full-orbed body ministry does not exist in many gatherings of believers.

It's good to keep in mind that the gifts of the Spirit are simply expressions of some facet of God's life through the believer. Actually, the literal translation of 1 Corinthians 12:1 is not "spiritual gifts" but "spirituals" or "spiritualities." And later in the chapter Paul refers to them as a "manifestation of the Spirit" (v. 7). Here the word literally means a shining forth of the Spirit or making the Spirit's actions visible. So all of this is closely tied in with God's overall purpose as we saw it earlier, "that the life of Jesus also may be manifested in our mortal flesh" (2 Corinthians 4:10). These expressions of the power of God are not to be regarded as "weird" any more than are the expressions of His love and peace. In fact, the gifts and the fruit of the Spirit are so much a part of one another that Paul spends a significant part of his major message on the gifts talking about love (1 Corinthians 12-14). The purpose of both is to express God's life.

Every major reference to the gifts of the Spirit makes it plain that these are for every believer as God sees fit to distribute them (Romans 12:6; 1 Corinthians 12:7; Ephesians 4:7). Even a superficial reading of these passages shows that their basic purpose is the building up of the church and that they are urgently needed for this purpose. Since the building of the church goes on until the day of the Lord, we can expect them to occur as a regular and normal part of church life until then, being exercised freely, and subject only to a few very reasonable boundaries and limitations. But since Satan is vigorously opposed to the building of the church, he has fought this expression of God's life by introducing into the minds of Christian men any number of strange ideas which cloud the simplicity of the teaching of the New Testament and render ineffective the ministry of God's people to His glory.

One common mistake is to confuse these gifts with natural talents which have been dedicated to God. By natural talents I mean those abilities which are ours by natural birth or which we develop by special training or education. Certainly natural talents should be completely committed to the Lord, and, when they are, God may be able to use them. But these are not the gifts of the Spirit to which Paul is referring. The manifestations of the Spirit can't be expressions of man's human soul-life. Of course they will be shaped by the vessel through whom they are expressed, but their source is in the Spirit. They become part of the believer's life when or after the Holy Spirit comes upon him in power for ministry.

First Corinthians 13:8-13 is often quoted to prove that

certain of the gifts have been done away with. The passage does say that there will be a day when the gifts will no longer be needed. But verse 10 tells us that this will be when "the perfect comes." Only Jesus is perfect, and if you compare 1 Corinthians 13:12 with 1 John 3:2, you will see that Paul is evidently referring to the day when we will see Jesus face to face and be made like Him. In that day, many things necessary here on earth will be replaced by things vastly superior. Love, of course, is the basic nature of God and will always exist. But today we need the gifts of the Spirit in full measure, expressed in love, for the building of His church. And today many of God's people are experiencing these things on a wider scale than has been seen for centuries. This is an exciting day to be serving God!

There is one other misconception which, though not so serious, is still confusing to some. I think it is caused by our understanding of the word *gift*. I think we sometimes get the idea that a "gift" of the Spirit is something God gives to an individual to have and to hold in himself and to use whenever he pleases. I don't think that is so, though some gifts, or manifestations, might occur often enough in one person's life to make it look like this is the case.

> *A gift of the Spirit is a grace-gift, a spiritual manifestation, a manifestation of the Holy Spirit through the believer. It is simply the Holy Spirit working through us in a given manner, at the time He, the Spirit, chooses, for the carrying out of the ministry to which we have been appointed by God. It is not something given us as a possession, but a privilege conferred of having the Holy Spirit use us as an instrument in certain ways and manifest His own power through us. This does not make the power manifested any less. It is power from on high. But it means that the power is not ours and does not function at our best and for our glory. It is manifested as we walk in full surrender and exercise full faith.*[1]

Of course, someone will object, "the gifts and the calling

of God are irrevocable" (Romans 11:29). Yes, but if you study that passage in context you will find that Paul is speaking of God's gifts to His entire body of people, not just to individuals. God will not take His gifts away from the church, but is He likely to put Himself in a position where He and His power can be manipulated by man? So He manifests His power through us in these miraculous ways, but does not give us gifts which we may use at any time. Instead, He moves to meet a need according to His sovereign will when the need is there. Another time when the same need occurs, He may use another member of His body to meet the need. So, one who has manifested gifts of healings cannot heal everyone at will, and so forth. Knowing and understanding this may help you to be more open and flexible toward the ministry of the Spirit through you.

The various ways the Spirit manifests Himself are described in the Bible by certain names given to the gifts. We're going to describe briefly each of them according to the categories provided by these names. But never forget that the Holy Spirit can't be put into a box. In actual practice, many times the expression of the Spirit will take the form of two or more gifts overlapping so that it's not always possible to say with certainty that "this is such and such a gift and that is so and so." The Spirit not a machine with seventeen different settings; He is a person and His life is the greatest and most varied in the universe. It's good to have some ideas of how these gifts operate, but we must retain a flexibility toward the sovereign working of God. Also remember that we are still coming out of the dark ages. The experienced men of the first century are not here to guide us, and we still have much to learn about these things. What I have to share is based upon study of the Scripture together with my own and others' experiences of seeing God successfully meet needs, but we should all be subject to further lessons the Lord may have for us in this and other areas. Also realize that seeming manifestations of the Spirit may be of the flesh or even counterfeited by Satan. Thus we need to learn to judge all manifestations by the Scriptures.

There are two basic passages which list gifts of the Spirit —Romans 12:6-8; and 1 Corinthians 12:8-10,28. To some extent, these lists overlap. For the purposes of explanation, we are going to rearrange the order of these slightly, but this new order is not intended to suggest any degrees of importance.

The nine manifestations in 1 Corinthians 12 are often the ones that raise the most questions, so we'll take them first. They fall rather easily into three categories:

Revelation gifts	Word of knowledge Word of wisdom Distinguishing of spirits
Power gifts	Gifts of healings The effecting of miracles Faith
Utterance gifts	Prophecy Various kinds of tongues Interpretation of tongues

The three revelation gifts are very similar and frequently overlap. They describe the work of the Spirit supernaturally revealing something directly from the all-knowing mind of God to the mind of man. God is omniscient; that is, He knows all there is to know about everything past, present, and future in both the physical and the spiritual world. When He wants to, He can reveal some item of this vast information to a human mind by the Spirit.

A word of knowledge, then, is not a good or unusual understanding of the Bible, or even that deep inner understanding of the ways of God which comes with maturity. It is not any form of knowledge that can be acquired by man through study or the use of his five senses. It is a direct revelation to a man of some fact from the mind of God. For instance, as I write this I have no idea of just where my brother is or what he is doing, but God knows. If He were to reveal it to me by the Spirit, that would be a word of knowledge.

A few of the many examples of this in Scripture might be Peter's knowledge of the hypocrisy of Ananias and Sapphira (Acts 5:1-4), the Spirit's revelation to Peter of the three men coming from Cornelius (Acts 10:19-20), and Agubus' disclosure of Paul's destiny in Jerusalem (Acts 21:11). These and other examples indicate that a word of knowledge can come either by a vision, a dream, or by a direct word to the mind.

A Christian businessman once came to me for spiritual counsel. His business was failing and he wondered if it might have some spiritual reason. He just wanted a Christian brother with whom he could share it and to counsel him. He spent nearly an hour explaining the details of his business and telling me how he had prayed and dedicated it to God. But the entire time he was talking, the words *his wife* kept coming to my mind. I wasn't even sure if he had a wife, but when he finished I looked at him and asked, "Jim, what about your wife?" "How did you know about that?" he asked, surprised. "Why don't you tell me about it?" I answered. He poured out a story of strife and division in his marriage that was leading to divorce, and confessed that much of it was his fault. Then I shared with him how I had known. The solution was obvious. He went to his wife, told her what had happened, and repented. She confessed to him as well, the marriage was saved, and his business began to prosper. All because of a crucial fact that I could never have known apart from God.

A word of knowledge doesn't mean that anyone knows all that God knows, or that he can be a seer anytime he desires. But it does mean that God is able to reveal what is needed in a supernatural way for His glory.

A word of wisdom is very similar, except that it deals more with a revelation from God as to what to do, or how to pray, rather than just a fact of knowledge. It is a supernatural unfolding of His plan and purpose for some particular situation, usually so that His servant can take the appropriate action to bring it to pass.

New Testament examples of a word of wisdom might include the angel's warning to Joseph about Herod's plan to destroy the Christ child (Matthew 2:13-14), the vision which sent Ananias to the blinded Saul in Damascus (Acts 9:10-18), the Spirit forbidding Paul and Silas from evangelizing in Asia (Acts 16:6), and the vision which sent them into Macedonia (Acts 16:9-10). Again, I think you can see that some of these are probably cases where the word of knowledge and the word of wisdom overlap.

My wife and I had a wonderful experience in which the Spirit was expressed in a Christian sister as the word of wisdom. One summer as we were traveling we encountered a situation which brought us great spiritual and emotional anguish. As a result of this situation we had two great needs about which we seemed unable to really pray in faith ourselves. In the midst of this trial, we were fellowshiping one evening with my wife's parents and another couple. Neither of these couples knew anything of these two specific needs; nor did they even know about the general situation. Yet as we were praying, this sister suddenly began to pray for us that God would meet these same two needs. She prayed so specifically that we were amazed at first. Then we realized that there was no way she could have known except that the Spirit had led her to pray by a word of wisdom. And beyond this, she prayed with such faith that the answers came in like a flood following her prayer. And our hearts were lifted up as again we realized that God is never limited to the boundaries of human understanding and ability.

Neither the word of knowledge or wisdom is necessarily vocal. We don't have to tell everything we know. Often it may be God's desire for us to be silent to others while either acting or praying concerning the situation ourselves. We should be especially careful if it seems that God has shown us something that someone else is to do. If He can show it to us, He can show it to them. We may be "in on it" so we can pray for them or to confirm it after they have revealed the direction they have received. But it is directly contrary to the teaching of Scripture for any man to become a mediator, or "middleman" between another and God (1 Timothy 2:5). This is sometimes done in the name of prophecy but, as we will see later, the gift of prophecy does not include this element.

Distinguishing of spirits (or "discerning of spirits," KJV) is also very much like a word of knowledge, except that the revelation given deals entirely with the discovery of demonic spirits rather than facts or incidents in the natural realm. There are many people about us who are possessed or oppressed by unclean, demonic spirits. We should never try to uncover their presence by "hunches," by guessing, or by "diagnosing" their symptoms. This will only result in people being labeled demon-possessed who really only have emotional problems or physical infirmities. It takes the Spirit to discern spirits. Also, this gift is not the gift of discernment. There is no such gift. Discerning of spirits does not enable one person to "discern" another's sins, but to recognize the presence of evil spirits. Neither is it the means of casting out those spirits. This would probably require other gifts in operation, such as faith and miracles.

Not long ago, a new convert brought a "Christian worker" to our home where we were having a Bible study with several other new Christians. The moment this man stepped in the house the Lord revealed to me that he was demon-possessed, but I waited for fifteen minutes or so while he gave his "testimony" of his own "salvation" and "work for the Lord." There was nothing in what he said to suggest that he was other than what he claimed. Finally, I looked right at him and denounced the evil spirit in him. The moment the spirit was discovered, the man's entire look and behavior changed. The spirit began to speak true to its own nature, cursing and blaspheming. Then the Lord showed us that there were two evil spirits, a religious spirit which caused the man to masquerade as a Christian worker, and an unclean spirit which caused him to be homosexual. He resisted our efforts to minister to him, thus refusing the deliverance which might have been his. But the Spirit's revelation was surely given to protect the gathering of Christians from the demonic influence. Some scriptural examples of this gift are Paul's encounter with Elymas, the sorcerer, and with the young woman in Philippi.

The purpose of the *gifts of healings* is obvious. It is for the supernatural healing of every kind of human disease and ill. Being supernatural, it has nothing to do with any recovery that may take place as the result of a physician's skill. Nor do we see it projected in Scripture in connection with men who hold large public meetings and take large offerings. Jesus said that the gifts of healings were freely given and that no true servant of God should ever profit financially because of them (Matthew 10:8). Also remember that this gift, like the others, is not given to a person to exercise whenever he will. If that were so, such a person ought to go to the hospitals and give himself to raising up the thousands who suffer. But it is not so. The Spirit manifests Himself in this way when, in His sovereign knowledge and will, God will be glorified and His Word confirmed in the proper way. Scriptural examples of this gift are so profuse in the gospels and in Acts that I'm not even going to list them here. Nor would it serve our purpose to comment on the whole subject of divine healing. That would take a book in itself. It's enough to say that God does heal men supernaturally today and that this involves the gifts of healings.

The effecting of miracles, or more literally, the "effects of works of power," is somewhat similar to the gifts of healings in that it brings about a supernatural change in a person or situation which can be easily observed and which will confirm God's Word and bring glory to Him. All healings are miracles, but not all miracles are healings. Miracles might range from restoring the lame man (Acts 3:6-7) to changing water into wine (John 2:1-11), from walking on the water (Matthew 14:25-29) to the sudden end of Ananias and Sapphira (Acts 5:5-10). This may have been the gift which was involved when cloths were taken from Paul's body in Ephesus to heal the sick (Acts 19:11-12). Throughout the book of Acts these special miracles occurred from time to time in order to confirm the Word of the Lord through His servants. And they are still happening today. A close friend of mine recently spent a year in Indonesia where God has been working in wondrous ways. He reports that in certain sections of that nation, many miracles have taken place, including nine well-documented cases of the dead being raised to life. The result has been the conversion of thousands of people, including a large percentage of Muslims, something that has never before taken place in the history of the Islamic religion.

Faith is the keystone for everything in the Christian life, as we have already pointed out earlier in the book. But the "gift" of faith referred to here is not the same as the "measure of faith" which the Lord has given to every man. It is not related to the faith that saves. Nor is it related to the faith that we exercise in trusting Christ each day for the supply of His life. The gift of faith is a special manifestation of the Spirit at the particular moment to give one of His servants faith above and beyond his usual capacity to believe God, so that that servant can trust Him to bring some special thing to pass. This gift probably works hand in hand with the effecting of miracles in the raising of the dead (Acts 20:9-12) or praying a brother out of jail (Acts 12:4-11). A student testified of an experience which may be an illustration of this gift in operation. On a number of religious college campuses lately there occurred a spontaneous revival. While visiting one of these colleges, this student heard someone give testimony to having had a short leg lengthened miraculously through prayer. My student friend had suffered all his life from the same problem, so when someone asked if he would like to be prayed for, he responded gladly. He shared with us that just as he was about to be prayed for, John 14:14 suddenly came into his mind: "If you ask Me anything in My name, I will do it." He stated that he felt God give him an absolute assurance that this verse applied to that specific situation. "I felt a degree of faith that I had never known before, nor have I really felt since, I just knew that God was going to heal me." It appears to me that God had given the gift of faith and of course the healing (or miracle) followed. His leg was instantaneously lengthened, to the glory of God.

Jesus' promise to confirm His Word with signs and wonders has often been forgotten. But the proper context for these amazing gifts is the ministry of the body of Christ and the lives of men whom He can trust to build according to His pattern. He has had precious few of these in past years, but I feel we are going to see an increase of these signs and wonders in the future if we stay focused on Christ and not on the miracles, and if we build for Him and not for man.

Because the utterance gifts occur more frequently, because they are more easily perverted and counterfeited, and because they are always vocal, God has imposed some controls upon them which He has not imposed on the other gifts.

The gift of prophecy is a much misunderstood gift. The word itself means to "speak forth." Because of this many have assumed that this gift relates to preaching and teaching. This is obviously not true since many women prophesied (Acts 21:9), but no woman was allowed to teach (1 Timothy 2:12). And preaching (Greek: telling good news), in the New Testament, has primarily to do with proclaiming the good news to unbelievers out where they are (Mark 16:15), whereas prophecy was a ministry to the church (1 Corinthians 14:4).

Prophecy is the enablement by the Spirit to speak out in a known language a word of edification without premeditation or preparation of the mind. In content, it is very similar to an interpretation of a tongue.

Prophecy in the New Testament church was not foretelling and it did not serve to give direction for another's life. Much harm has been done by people "prophesying" over one another, stating that God was sending them off to the mission field, and so forth. All of this kind of soulish excess and satanic imitation could be eliminated if Christians would simply follow the plain teaching of the Word of God regarding this gift. There are two verses in 1 Corinthians 14 which ought to be carefully studied in connection with this. Verse 29 tells us that every prophecy is to be judged. And verse 3 gives the guidelines for that judgment: "One who prophesies speaks to men for edification and exhortation and consolation." And that's it! Obviously, revealing the "mind of God" for another individual does not fit into these categories, nor does revelation of new doctrine. Prophecy does not reveal anything new, but it only reminds us of what God has already stated in His Word, speaking of His promises, His faithfulness, and encouraging us to serve and trust Him.

It's good to realize the difference between *prophecy* and the *prophet*. Paul said that all may prophesy (1 Corinthians 14:31), but that not all were prophets (1 Corinthians 12:29). We can assume that prophets did prophesy, but they also had a much more far-ranging ministry of laying the foundation of the church and manifesting many other gifts of the Spirit. Prophets were severely judged in both the Old and New Testaments if found false, but in the church it was the prophecies, not the person, that were judged. If a brother prophesies and the church judges him to be in the flesh, he is to be helped and ministered to, not cast out (unless he refuses to be helped). Prophecy can serve a wonderful purpose of encouraging the saints and stimulating their faith, but it is always subject to the one exercising it

(1 Corinthians 14:32) and he in turn must be subject to the restrictions of the Word of God regarding it.

Speaking in *"various kinds of tongues"* is also an utterance gift and one that is much misunderstood. One very faulty concept of this gift is that it is to equip missionaries to speak the language of the people to whom they are going to minister. This concept has no scriptural basis, though some would relate it to the events in Acts 2. The facts are that most of the crowd gathered on the day of Pentecost would have understood the universal language of the Roman Empire, Greek, as well as their own native language. Also most of them would have understood either Hebrew or Aramaic, being mostly Jews who had returned to Jerusalem for the feast days. Apparently they understood Peter's explanation of the matter without supernatural help. So no supernatural gift would have been required if simple communication was all that was required. The "tongues" given that day were explained by Peter as a supernatural sign that Jesus had been exalted and prophecy fulfilled. It was a miracle to confirm the word preached, not a convenience to help the Christians communicate. Also remember that Paul says "tongues" are always to be accompanied by interpretation (1 Corinthians 14:27-28). This would never be necessary if the one speaking in tongues were already speaking the language of the people to whom he was ministering. Speaking in tongues has nothing to do with missionary linguistics.

Speaking in tongues is the enablement by the Spirit to speak in a language unknown to the speaker, and for the most part, unknown to his listeners. There are two basic purposes for this ability mentioned in Scripture. One of these is for private use, the other for the church.

Paul says that "one who speaks in a tongue does not speak to men, but to God; for no one understands, but in his spirit he speaks mysteries" (1 Corinthians 14:2). What does this mean? It means that the Spirit of God enables my spirit to commune directly with God, bypassing my very limited understanding. "In the same way the Spirit also helps our weaknesses; for we do not know how to pray as we should, but the Spirit Himself intercedes for us with groanings too deep for words" (Romans 8:26). Surpassing the limitation of the human mind in praise, worship, and petition to God is very edifying at times (1 Corinthians 14:4). (Of course, we are to "pray with the understanding" also.) But this phase of the ministry of tongues is different from the gift as it is expressed for the edification of the church. First Corinthians 14:4 says that a man who speaks in a tongue edifies himself. Any believer can pray to God in a tongue as he is enabled by the Spirit, but only those who are especially anointed at the time should use that gift to minister to the church.

The ministry to the church is always accompanied by interpretation or it is of no value to the church and not worth taking time away from other edifying ministries (1 Corinthians 14:5-13, 26-28). Since a message in a tongue with interpretation is equal to prophecy (1 Corinthians 14:5), the same controls are imposed by the Word. Three instances in a single meeting are enough (1 Corinthians 14:27), and all of it is to be judged by 1 Corinthians 14:3 (cf. 1 Corinthians 14:29).

Interpretation of tongues is simply the enablement by the Spirit to give the sense or meaning of the tongue that was uttered. It is not a translation of the language, but simply conveys the essence of what was said in the tongue. It is not a natural ability to understand the language spoken, but an utterance given by the Spirit following a tongue. In content and appearance it is very similar to prophecy.

In Romans 12, the first charismatic gift mentioned is prophecy (verse 6), which has already been mentioned in Corinthians. Also in Romans are listed several gifts which I call "the love gifts." Of course, all of the gifts are to be expressed in love, but these have the special expression of love bound up in what they are. These love gifts are rather similar to one another and might be hard to label when observed.

Serving (ministering, KJV) means to take the attitude and role of a servant to another. Jesus was manifesting this gift when He washed the feet of the disciples (compare John 13:5 with Matthew 20:28). Timothy and Erastus were described as manifesting this gift toward Paul (Acts 19:22).

Giving means literally to share something or to impart something to another. This can be imparting either something material or something spiritual. In the case of imparting something spiritual, this gift would probably operate along wtih another gift such as teaching, or faith. Paul wanted to go to Rome so that he could "impart" some spiritual gifts to them (Romans 1:11). In sharing materially, this gift would probably apply where the Spirit gives extraordinary grace to give to another sacrificially and beyond the usual.

Showing mercy is not just a matter of feeling sorry for someone. It is an active act, usually having to do with forgiveness (Matthew 18:27-33). In the close and intimate contact of body life, there is ample need and opportunity for this gift, for you will probably be personally wronged many times (Ephesians 4:32). According to Jude, this gift is especially helpful toward those who are having real spiritual problems and who seem to be slipping away into sin (Jude 22-23). So often these people are judged harshly by the self-righteous, when they could be helped by a display of mercy.

One other "love gift" is mentioned in 1 Corinthians 12:28: *helps.* The literal meaning is "to lay hold of to support." It is very close to showing mercy as it seems primarily to have to do with helping the weak. "Admonish the unruly, encourage the fainthearted, help the weak, be patient with all men" (1 Thessalonians 5:14).

Leading (ruleth, KJV) (Romans 12:8) and *administrations* (governments, KJV) (1 Corinthians 12:28) are gifts which apply most directly to the work of the elders, though at various times other Christians may manifest such a gift. The word *ruleth* in the King James Version is a poor translation, for one with this gift does not rule as a king. He is not the "head" of the church. Nor does it mean that he "leads" the meetings. He leads the church by what he is as well as what he does (see 1 Corinthians 11:1; Titus 2:7). The word literally means "to go before to lead." It is a real gift to be used by the Spirit so that others can see the mind of the Lord in a matter as expressed in the actions of a sound leader.

Two other gifts are mentioned in Romans. *Teaching* is the enablement by the Spirit to explain the Word of God. It differs from a gift such as prophecy in that it does not have the same spontaneous character. The very nature of the gift demands serious preparation and careful study. With this type of gift one is seldom unexpectedly anointed to minister, but will have spent much time before the Lord and in the Scripture searching out the truths God has given in a specific area. Of course the study cannot be a mere matter of accumulating head knowledge without a real quickening of the Spirit, but that does not negate the fact that much study is involved.

The gift of teaching is a very vital one to the local church. The Scriptures are the basis for judging all of the other gifts and for judging doctrine as well. Unless there is a strong ministry of teaching within the fellowship, it is very easy for error and mistakes to creep in. This is already happening in many little groups across the country. In many cases it is because there are none in the group who will discipline themselves to the labor of teaching. Paul gives an indication of the value of this ministry when he says to give double honor to the elders who work hard at it (1 Timothy 5:17). Another indication of the weight of this ministry is given by James: "Let not many of you become teachers, my brethren, knowing that as such we shall incur a stricter judgment" (James 3:1). The task of teaching eternal truths is an awesome one which should never be taken lightly.

As we mentioned earlier, it's regrettable that in the institutional church the ministry of teaching has sometimes become so dominant that it has squeezed out most other gifts and ministries. But we must not allow ourselves to react to this by underemphasizing this essential ministry. If the Lord is allowed to be head of His church, there will be plenty of time and opportunity for teaching together with the rich variety of other ministries. And in these last days, while deception grows and the world is in chaos, there is perhaps a greater need than ever before for God to raise up sound teachers who will help lay the foundation for the new wineskins of the twentieth century.

Exhortation is the gift of encouraging someone to pursue some particular course of conduct in the future. It is not always a ministry to the group, but can equally be a ministry to an individual.

When Paul writes about the charismatic gifts, he gives both warnings and encouragements. It's good to be aware of both and not to become unbalanced in either direction. It's obvious that such gifts do not make anyone "spiritual." The Corinthian church was not lacking in any (charismatic) gift (1 Corinthians 1:4-7), yet they were described as carnal (1 Corinthians 3:1-3). However, that was not the fault of the gifts but the fault of the Corinthians. You see, gifts can be used without love (1 Corinthians 13:1-3), and they can be used to create confusion (1 Corinthians 14:23). I can't tell you how or why this is so, but if it were not so, Paul s letter to the Corinthians would never have been written. Paul also warns that gifts do not make one infallible. What the Spirit says will be true, of course, but there is always the possibility of the flesh getting in on the act, and of satanic imitation. That's why we are to judge (1 Corinthians 14:29), especially the utterance gifts. Paul also states that the spirits of the prophets are subject to the prophets (1 Corinthians 14:32). This means that no one can ever say that he was acting under the compulsion of the Spirit and could not help what he was doing. If he was under the compulsion of a spirit, it was not the Holy Spirit. The Holy Spirit will never do anything or cause anyone to do anything contrary to the Word of God. All spiritual manifestations should be judged as to whether they adhere to the Word of God in all aspects (1 John 4:1). If they do not, they are not expressions of God's Spirit.

On the other hand, Paul's solution for the problems in the Corinthian church was not to ban the gifts. This is the course which has been taken by so many. It is an attempt to solve a spiritual problem with a carnal solution, and it does not help. Far from banning the gifts, Paul specifically writes at length so they won't be ignorant of the gifts (1 Corinthians 12:1). He could have banned the gifts with one sentence. We are commanded not to despise gifts, (1 Thessalonians 5:19-20) but to earnestly desire them (1 Corinthians 12:31; 14:1), and to stir up those we have (2 Timothy 1:6). And he plainly states, "Do not forbid to speak in tongues" (1 Corinthians 14:31). There is such a great need for balance in this area among God's people. In the past, most of us have either panicked and run from the issue, or climbed on one hobby horse and ridden it to death. In the future, let's yield our members as instruments of righteousness to God (Romans 6:13) and let Him create the balanced, functioning body He desires!

What does all of this have to do with you and me? God has chosen us to express His life in this old world. The fruit of the Spirit is part of it, and the gifts of the Spirit are part of it. Without both, the church, as God desires it, is impossible and the purpose of God is frustrated. Paul says to "pursue love, yet desire earnestly spiritual gifts" (1 Corinthians 14:1). God has some wonderful new experiences for you as you make yourself available to Him and all that He has for you. Walk in the Spirit, keep using the faith He has given you, and expect Him to use you continually. Before gathering with the Christians, pray that God will use you and show you just where you fit as a functioning part of the body. Keep your eye on the Giver and the gifts will follow!

14

"THE HOLY SPIRIT HAS MADE YOU OVERSEERS"

And when they had appointed elders for them in every church, having prayed with fasting, they commended them to the Lord in whom they had believed (Acts 14:23).

A local expression of the body of Christ is a wonderful organism, designed by God with the purpose that everyone in it would function fully under the direct leading of the Spirit of God. But God is not naive. He knows that there will always be in the church young Christians, new converts, and even older Christians who have spiritual problems, who sometimes walk in the flesh and who need the ministry and help of more mature brothers who have already experienced the same problems and have found Christ to be the answer. That's why He has appointed elders in every church.

"Who is the pastor of your church?" This question, asked so often, is an indication of the confusion surrounding the subject of leadership in the local church. Very few believers today actually understand the New Testament provision for local leadership, yet it is essential if we are to see a true expression of body, life and ministry.

One confusing factor is the terminology. Pastor, bishop, presbyter, overseer, elder are among the terms used. "Bishop" and "overseer" are simply different translations of the same Greek word. "Elder" and "presbyter" are also the same word in the Greek. Titus 1:5-7 makes it plain that "elder" and "overseer" are two names which apply to the same task and the same man. Acts 20:17, 28 show that it is the elders, or overseers, who do the pastoral work. So, scripturally, all of these terms apply to the same men and not to five distinct offices. God has made only one provision for the oversight and shepherding of the local church and that provision is the local elders. But what is an elder? Well, the word itself is probably the best description. Elders are simply the more mature among the local believers. The word is relative, of course. I doubt that the elders in Iconium appointed by Paul and Barnabas on their first trip were as mature as the elders appointed by Timothy in Ephesus. Those Iconium elders were only a few months old in the Lord, whereas those in Ephesus had had three years with Paul and more time with Timothy. But the Iconium elders were "elder" among the brothers in Iconium. The basic qualification for elders is that they be more mature than the other local brothers. The heart of their ministry is to watch over the younger, helping them to grow.

Of course, there are other qualifications. These are listed in 1 Timothy 3:1-7; Titus 1:5-9; and 1 Peter 5:1-4. An elder must be:

1. Above reproach and an example in all things to the believers.
2. The husband of one wife. That wife is to be dignified, temperate, faithful, and not a gossip.
3. A good father whose children obey and respect him. These children should be believers if they are old enough.
4. Hospitable. His home should be open to the local Christians, to the traveling brothers, and even to strangers.
5. Temperate and self-controlled. Not addicted to wine, etc. Prudent and gentle. Not stubborn or self-willed. Does not arge and brawl. Sensible, just, devout and a lover of good.
6. Have a respectable reputation in the community.
7. Free from the love of money.
8. Eagerly and voluntarily overseeing the flock without a desire for power over others, but only to please God.

9. Not a new convert. A new convert might become conceited.
10. Have ability to teach, though that doesn't have to be his only ministry in the body. Must have ability in the Word to exhort believers and to refute the false teachers.

I think that you can see that these qualifications are simply a description of a mature Christian who is walking in the Spirit and expressing the life of Christ. Elders are not super-saints. They are not highly qualified and trained specialists. They are not in a class by themselves. They are just good brothers in the Lord who, like all the others, have various ministries in the body. But in addition, they are more mature than the others and have been given a special responsibility to watch over the others and help them along.

There are four things in particular which are common to all New Testament elders which, if noted, will help to clear up a lot of the confusion concerning local church leadership.

1. Elders in the local church are always multiple in number. That is, there were always several, never only one, in each local church. In every instance in the New Testament where elders in the local church are mentioned they are plural in number (Acts 14:23; 15:2; 20:17; 21:17-18; Phillipians 1:1; Titus 1:5; James 5:14; 1 Peter 5:1). There is not a single exception to this and there was never intended to be any for the entire church age.

We don't have a record of every church established by the first-century apostles any more than we have a record of every word they preached. But the Holy Spirit has recorded examples of both in the Acts to give us an accurate and thorough description of both their message and their methods. Barnabas and Paul's first trip as apostles gives us a record of the appointing of elders. These men traveled to several cities, evangelizing in each city and teaching the believers for a short time. Then they went on to the next city. After a few months of this, they returned to each of the cities where there were groups of believers, and they "appointed elders for them in every church" (Acts 14:23). Many years and much experience later, Paul still urged Titus to do the same (Titus 1:5). God had shown these men His plan and they stuck by it.

There is one problem with this plan. It was expressed to me just a few days ago by a denominational pastor. We were talking about small-group meetings and he said, "It works OK in the beginning, but sooner or later a leader will come to the surface and take over. That's just human nature." He's right, of course. But the church is not intended to run by human nature, but by God's nature. Man's perverted nature, and the entire principle and spirit of Antichrist, is to raise up a single man to power and preeminence over other men. But God's nature in a man causes him to love and share and be humble. Wherever God's Spirit is allowed to lead, you will find expression of the interdependence of the body, even among the leadership of plural elders.

To place the responsibility in the hands of several brethren rather than in the hands of one individual, is God's way of safeguarding His Church against the evils that result from the domination of a strong personality. God has purposed that several brothers should unitedly bear responsibility in the church, so that even in controlling its affairs they have to depend upon one another and submit one to another. Thus in an experimental way they will have opportunity to give practical expression to the truth of the Body of Christ. As they honor one another and trust one another to the leading of the Spirit, none taking the place of the Head, but each regarding the others as fellow members, the element of "mutuality" which is the peculiar feature of the Church, will be preserved. *[1]

It didn't take long for some churches to begin to stray from this simple principle. But wherever they did, it caused real problems and was denounced by the Lord through the apostles (3 John 9-10; Revelation 2:6, 15-16). Today the usual thing is a professional pastor who works with a "board" of local elders, or a group of elders, one of whom is recognized as the "chief" elder. But the simplicity of God's plan calls for a group of local brothers who share equally the yoke of the Lord, submitting to one another and humbly leading the church by the example of their lives (1 Peter 5:3).

2. Elders in the local church are always local men. There is a definite place for workers who travel about from place to place building up the churches, as we will see in chapter 16, but their place is not in the leadership of the local church. That responsibility was for local men who truly represented the local expression of the body of Christ in that area. Elders are not something apart from and above the local church; they are part of the local church and therefore they must be local men. Again, every passage dealing with the appointment of elders agrees with this, and there is not a single instance in Scripture of anyone being imported to an area to become an elder in the local church.

Of course, some feel that Timothy and Titus were sent to Ephesus and Crete to become local church leaders. In fact, the King James Version adds a note after 2 Timothy and after Titus which refers to these men as the first bishops of their areas. But this note is not part of the inspired text and was added in 1611. The fact is that both Timothy and Titus were sent to appoint local men as elders and were both about to travel on to other areas when those letters were written by Paul to them.

I've heard others say that the apostles only appointed local men in those early years because they had no trained pastors to bring in. But this is not so. Even at the time of Paul and Barnabas' first trip, there were seasoned, mature men back at both Jerusalem and Antioch (Acts 13:1; 15:4). Why didn't they send for these men instead of appointing local men who were less than six months old in the Lord? Because they knew God's plan and bowed to the wisdom of it! They also knew that it doesn't take long for men who are living by Christ and ministering to one another regularly to mature.

The wisdom of it should be apparent to everyone. Local men know and are genuinely concerned about the local people. The local church will never suddenly find itself without pastoral ministry because someone has been promoted or has received a call to a bigger church. But the heart of it lies simply in what the local church is—the Christians of the area gathered in the name of the Lord to express His life. That's all it takes to have a local church, and there is simply no need for anyone extra-local in the picture.

3. Elders in the local church are not paid for their ministry. In other words, they were what we would call laymen. Because there were always several elders in each local church, because each church was kept small in number, and because these men were already local there was no need for them to give up their regular occupations to serve as elders. In fact, for them to do so might very well endanger not only them, but the local church as well.

"The love of money is a root of all sorts of evil, and some by longing for it have wandered away from the faith, and have pierced themselves with many a pang" (1 Timothy 6:10). This statement gives the reason for the principle in this matter. One of Paul's chief contentions was with teachers who began to teach false doctrine because they found they could make it pay (Titus 1:10-11).

The passage which is invariably quoted in support of the idea of salaried leaders is 1 Timothy 5:17-18: "Let the elders who rule well be considered worthy of double honor, especially those who work hard at preaching and teaching. For the Scripture says, 'You shall not muzzle the ox while he is threshing, 'and the laborer is worthy of his wages'." Timothy, who knew the principle of God in this matter, could never have connected these verses in such a way as to think Paul was saying "give the elders who teach and evangelize double salary." The larger context of the chapter shows that Paul is speaking about honor, not salary. The next thing he refers to is the matter of not allowing easy accusations against elders (1 Timothy 5:19) and after that he warns Timothy not to appoint anyone hastily (1 Timothy 5:22).

Peter was firm on this, as well: "Therefore, I exhort the elders among you,. . .shepherd the flock of God among you, not under compulsion, but voluntarily, *according to the will of God; and not for sordid gain,* but with eagerness" (1 Peter 5:1-2). No doubt Peter remembered Jesus' words: "He who is a hireling, and not a shepherd, who is not the owner of the sheep, beholds the wolf coming, and leaves the sheep, and flees, and the wolf snatches them, and scatters them. He flees because he is a hireling, and is not concerned about the sheep" (John 10:12-13).

Paul told the elders at Ephesus:

Be on guard for yourselves and for all the flock, among which the Holy Spirit has made you overseers, to shepherd the church of God which He purchased with His own blood. I know that after my departure savage wolves will come in among you, not sparing the flock; and from among your own selves men will arise, speaking perverse things, to draw away the disciples after them (Acts 20:28-30).

I have coveted no one's silver or gold or clothes. You yourselves know that these hands ministered to my own needs and to the men who were with me. In every thing I showed you that by working hard in this manner you must help the weak and remember the words of the Lord Jesus, that He Himself said, "It is more blessed to give than to receive" (Acts 20:33-35).

A multitude of problems will be avoided if elders and churches abide by this principle, especially the problem that occurs when people get the idea that they are paying someone else to "do the job" and conclude that they can lay back and retire themselves. This is just what has happened throughout the church today.

The plain principle, then, is for elders to work for their own living and shepherd the church in their free time. Of course, it is the privilege of an elder or any other Christian to give up secular employment for a time in order to give himself more fully to some aspect of the Lord's work if the Spirit should so lead. But his income during this time must be truly by faith (Hebrews 11:6): not making his needs known, not taking up offerings, not soliciting for funds directly or by letter, and above all, not presuming the local church into the bondage of having to support him. (See chapters 16 and 17 on Faith and Finance.)

We have two men in our fellowship in Chicago, each with a wife and children. One man works two days a week at a secular job, while the other works three days a week. Each looks to God to supply the rest of what is necessary to meet the needs of themselves and their families. One of these men has done this for several years now, sometimes holding no secular job at all. Both men feel God has specifically led them to live this way for the present time so they can give extra time to prayer, study of the Word, evangelism, and the work of the Lord. The proof of this is that God has supplied their needs. But they have not been dependent upon the church. In fact, nearly all of their support comes from outside our little fellowship, and the fact that they live this way is not related in any way to their positions or ministries in the church. It is simply something between them and God. If He has led them to give up secular employment to be available to Him, then He must supply their needs. And so it would be for any other brother in a local church, whether he was an elder or not. For those whom the Spirit leads this way, He will supply. Those who are not truly led by the Spirit will discover it rather quickly if they are careful not to make their needs known to men in any way. If it is truly a work of pure faith, God will be glorified. But all of this has no connection with a man's specific responsibilities as elder, and could never be construed as salary for that purpose.

4. The elders in the local church have the pastoral ministry of the church. I've already referred to this several times, but I want you to see it in the light of two basic passages of Scripture.

The word *pastor* only occurs one time in the New Testament, in Ephesians 4:11. But the function of pastoring is described both by Peter and by Paul.

> *Therefore I exhort the elders among you,. . .shepherd the flock of God (1 Peter 5:1-2).*
>
> *And from Miletus he sent to Ephesus and called to him the elders of the church. And when they had come to him, he said to them,. . ."Be on guard for yourselves and for all the flock, among which the Holy Spirit has made you overseers, to shepherd the church of God" (Acts 20:17-28).*

These two passages make it abundantly clear that it is the responsibility of the local elders to shepherd, or pastor, the flock. We cannot imagine that God ever intended for these elders to hire someone, either an outsider or one of their own number, to do that pastoral work. Nor can we gather that this pastoral work is the responsibility of only one of the elders, for all the elders are clearly charged with it. Whatever else their individual ministries might be, prophet, teacher, evangelist, healer, or whatever, as elders they carry the responsibility of pastoring the church together.

Modern practice has made us associate this pastoral work with pulpit "preaching" (which is usually really more like the New Testament ministry of teaching). But while an elder should have ability to teach, and that may even be his primary ministry, it is not necessarily so. Elders are not "the ministers" of the church who stand to teach while others remain passively in their seats. They do minister, but so do all of the other saints, while the elders oversee the body as it functions.

How does an elder actually function, then? Well, if you

were to visit a gathering of the believers you would probably not be able to tell who the elders were. They are seated mingled in with the other believers. Their ministries in the gathering may be as diverse as anyone else's. If someone were severely out of order, they might step in and lovingly but firmly bring things back into order. But often their ministry as elders takes place outside of the gatherings as they seek out the weak and stumbling to counsel with them; as they help new believers to learn to pray, study the Word, and to live by Christ; as they reconcile brothers who have wronged one another; and as they rebuke those who are stubbornly going astray. They are shepherds. The basic ministry as a shepherd is not to give sermons but to care for sheep.

Where do they come from? As we have seen, they were appointed by the apostles in the churches planted by the apostles. But the apostles were only appointing, or recognizing those whom the Holy Spirit had already chosen. "The Holy Spirit has made you overseers" (Acts 20:28). An "elder" is a man as well as an office. It takes the work of the Spirit to make the man. Only when the Spirit gives him the gifts and tries his faith to refine him to maturity can men recognize him as elder. When the Spirit has done this, it will be evident to all the church and not just to the apostles.

There don't seem to be many true apostles among the churches today. I do expect God to raise up some in the future out of the many little fellowship groups being born around the world. We need to be much in prayer that the Lord will send out laborers, men of real apostolic ministry who can lay a strong foundation. In the meantime, God will make evident those who have the pastoral ministry of elders in each local church. No one will have to seek the office, and no "elections" need to be held. Nor does a group have to regard itself as less than a church simply because no apostle has recognized elders in their midst. As God equips men with the gifts and maturity, let their brothers and sisters in the Lord honor them accordingly and this will be sufficient so far as I can see. No "official appointment" will make them more or less able to shepherd the flock of God. And there is no need to hurry, either. If haste was dangerous in Ephesus when Timothy was there (1 Timothy 5:22), how much more so today. I know of one church where they got eager to have elders. They appointed five and since then three more. But today only two are left in the church just eight months after the first five were appointed. God is building a living church from living stones, and that takes time. Surely we have as much time as He!

All of this may sound a little formal and legalistic. But it doesn't have to be that way. Just remember that we are still talking about the form that the life of God wants to take spontaneously in His body. If the Spirit is allowed to truly lead, all these things will come to pass easily and naturally. The church is still the same sweet simplicity of a few believers gathered together to love one another, but now we've learned that among them will be some to whom the Spirit has given a special heart to watch over the younger and weaker so that we might all become like Jesus in every way. These are simply older brothers in the family of God, the elders who will love and shepherd us until the Chief Shepherd returns in His glory.

15

LOVING MEN TO CHRIST

Evangelism is where it all started for me. Since the day I became a Christian, I've been concerned with the witness of the "laymen." It was during the struggle to get the people of God mobilized to evangelize that I really began to ask some objective questions about the church. It just seemed that we couldn't really get people concerned and out doing the job, at least not in sufficient numbers. I say "we" because I can name at least a dozen or more other men who were in the same boat and who, as a result, had come to pretty much the same conclusions. Most of us were convinced that evangelism was the ultimate objective of God and we fought and worked hard to see it come to pass. We continually asked questions. What actually is evangelism? How is it to be done? Who is suppose to be doing it? Why aren't we getting it done? And, What is the matter with the church when it produces so many Christians who are unable to share their faith?

A lot of water has passed under the bridge since them. Now I think of the ultimate purpose of God for man as something quite different. It seems clear to me that God wants a people who live by His life so that they might express His nature and bring glory to Him. Evangelism is not the ultimate purpose of God, but it is fundamentally important to the purpose of God. Don't ever lose sight of the importance of evangelism, but seek to keep it in balance with the other things God is doing as well.

The real key is to understand evangelism as one of the spontaneous by-products of the life of God being lived out in an individual. In other words, evangelism is a normal part of the ministry of every man in whom the Spirit of God dwells. It is God loving men through me. In chapter 10, I mentioned this in connection with 2 Corinthians 5:17-19. I'd like you to look at these verses again.

> *Therefore if any man is in Christ, he is a new creature; the old things passed away; behold, new things have come. Now all these things are from God, who reconciled us to Himself through Christ, and gave us the ministry of reconciliation, namely, that God was in Christ reconciling the world to Himself.*

For us, the beginning is when God reconciles us (brings us back) to Himself. But not only us—the entire world! Big job! What was His method? "God was in Christ reconciling . . . ." Every moment of Jesus' recorded life was an expression of the life and love of God. Why? Because for thirty years He had lived by the life of the Father within Him (Hebrews 5:8; John 5:19; 14:10). Then He simply made Himself available to the Father and began to walk (by faith) through a small corner of the world. The spontaneous result is called "the ministry of reconciliation"—the Spirit of God loving men to Himself through a submitted human soul and body. And the Bible says that God has now given this "ministry" to "us." Who is *us? Us* is "any man. . .in Christ." *US* is you and I—people with a "new thing," the life of God within and bursting to get out.

And that's why evangelism is never something you "should do." Evangelism is something you are, if you are living by Christ. And the motivation is not primarily the "command" of the Great Commission. Neither is the basic motivation for evangelism the emotional plea to help the dying millions. (That's too abstract and far away: "For me to love the whole world is no chore; my only problem is my neighbor next door!") No, Paul says it's simply that "the love of Christ controls us" (2 Corinthians 5:14). And when the love of Christ controls us we love the one next door, the person in the office, or the roommate at school with a love that woos them to Jesus. And that's not a "job" and it doesn't take a committee—it's life and it works!

Many people are under the impression that it was the apostles, especially Paul, who evangelized the Roman Empire for Christ. Actually, for the first eight years or so, there was little evangelism anywhere but in Jerusalem. The Christians were gathered there, learning to live by Christ. Then Saul's persecution scattered them, that is, all of them except the apostles, who stayed in Jerusalem. "Those who had been scattered went about preaching the word" (Acts 8:4). Everywhere they went they shared with their neighbors or fellow tradesmen, and little knots of Christians began to appear in almost every town and city. Now, some of these who were scattered had been evangelists already in Jerusalem, such as Philip and Stephen. But the vast majority were simply sharers of life and, wherever they went, people learned about Jesus Christ.

We're not told very much about the evangelists in the New Testament. It's obvious that they had a special ministry of bringing others to Christ. In Ephesians 4:11-12, we're also told that they are among those who are to help equip the saints to do the work of the ministry. As evangelists, part of their ministry to the church was to help the other believers develop their own effectiveness in sharing Christ. Apparently, some of them remained primarily local in their ministries. Philip's ministry in Samaria, for instance, may have taken place while he was traveling from his ex-home in Jerusalem to his new home in Caesarea where he lived for many years afterward (Acts 8:4-5,40; 21:8). Others may have traveled as full-time itinerant evangelists with some of the apostles (Acts 16:1-3; 2 Timothy 4:5). But there is no basis for thinking of them as men who traveled about the country, holding "revival" meetings in church buildings, preaching to crowds who are mostly Christian, and taking "love offerings" for their support.

Whatever the role of the evangelist in the early church, still it was the ordinary believers who did the bulk of the evangelism. Paul, Silas, and Timothy spent a very short time in Thessalonica and left behind a little group of new believers (Acts 17:1-9). But only eighteen months later, Paul wrote to them to commend them because the Word of the Lord had spread throughout Greece from their little church (1 Thessalonians 1:2-8). Probably the love of God in their lives not only made an impact on the other local citizens, but on those traveling through as well. This is a wonderful example of how a local church, just by being what God wants it to be, can make a great impact on the world for Jesus Christ.

There wasn't much method to the evangelism of the early church, but there was one basic principle which has been ignored somewhat in our day. The principle was that evangelism, whether mass or personal, was *always* done out where the people were. Since it was a matter of spontaneous life, and not a matter of following some institutionally structured method, they simply shared wherever they encountered people who would listen. If they encountered an individual, they shared with an individual. If they came across a crowd, they shared with a crowd. But it never even occurred to them to invite people to the meetings of the church to hear the good news. That would have violated two other basic principles of the Christian life: (1) That the Spirit of God is always within the Christian, equipping him for ministry wherever he is, and (2) that the gatherings of the church were family meetings intended for believers only, where each could share in liberty with his brothers and sisters in the Lord.

In our day, many have resorted to inviting their neighbor to church because they have not experienced the Spirit of God coming upon them in power. With little to share, yet under pressure to evangelize the world, the only alternative is the church-invitation method. This in turn has made it almost impossible to have real believers' meetings because the constant presence of unbelievers makes it necessary to maintain certain forms and controls.

Compare today's evangelism with the New Testament and you'll quickly see that the Reformation was not a complete "restoration." The primary means of evangelism today was entirely unknown in the first century. *The "come to church" method of evangelism is often evasive, largely unfruitful and unscriptural.* Have you ever stopped to think that when a believer attempts to evangelize his neighbor by inviting him to church, he is in effect saying, "Neighbor, you desperately need spiritual life. But I have none to give, so you'll have to come with me to someone who does." What a terrible admission for a believer after Jesus said, "He who believes in me. . .from his innermost being shall flow rivers of living water" (John 7:38). God does not dwell in a place, but in men. *You have life to share wherever you are!*

Then add to that the fact that only a small percentage of the Americans who are not now Christians will probably ever come to church even if invited. And of those who do come, only a fraction respond. That means that most of the population is doomed just because Christians limit themselves to "come" evangelism. Consider the adjustments an unbeliever has to make to come to church. He feels about as comfortable and at home as you would in a Communist cell meeting. I think he has a right to hear the gospel on his own territory, man to man—not outnumbered three or four hundred to one. Let's be willing to go to people where they are and adjust to them as we share life with them.

We must get hold of the fact that "come" evangelism is basically unscriptural. The pattern of the early church has been given to us as a description of the way the life of God behaves in men committed to Him and His ways. There is not a single instance of anyone being invited to any meeting for the purpose of evangelizing him. Every instance of evangelism, both mass and personal, took place in the ordinary environment of the unbelievers. There is a great need today for the people of God simply to be out in the world loving and witnessing to people, and for evangelists and apostles to carry out their evangelistic efforts out where the unbelievers are, in accord with the New Testament pattern.

The normal place that you should expect God to use you is right where you are in the regular course of your everyday living. If you can't share Christ with those around you now, going somewhere else won't help. Businessmen take charter flights to Europe, students make mass treks to Florida, and other believers go month after month to a skid-row mission —many with the hope that they would somehow be more effective among strangers than they are among those who know them. Others quit their jobs or drop out of school to go to Africa or South America when they have never won a single individual to Christ here at home. I don't mean to say that there may not be a place for special evangelistic efforts like these at times, but if the going is simply to escape the reality of ineffectiveness where you are, there is not likely to be much fruit where you are going, either.

Of course, if you don't normally encounter unbelievers in the regular pattern of your everyday living, you may have to make some adjustments. One lady shared with me that she was a housewife and her only contacts outside her home were with the people in her church. I suggested that she spend one evening a week at the YWCA taking a flower-arranging class or something like that. She did and found a ready-made mission field of thirty lonely, frustrated people the first night she entered the classroom.

The world is filled with people who have a desperate need for a friend, for someone to talk to, for someone to share their fears with. Set aside one evening a month to invite a neighbor family over for dinner. Take a business associate to lunch, not to discuss business but just to get acquainted with him as a person. Join the PTA or become a room mother at your children's school. Include in your golf game the fellow you're praying for.

It may very well be that you'll spend several visits with an individual before ever having an opportunity to share anything spiritual. Or the subject may come up at once. But don't be tense about it. Just remember that Christ lives in you. Let Him control your life and the rest will follow. Make yourself available to God and to people and you'll be surprised how easily and frequently you'll be able to share Christ.

When I say that evangelism is simply spontaneously loving others, I don't mean that this love is only demonstrated and never spoken. There is a great need for a demonstration of the love of God to others in daily living, and most evangelism starts there. But to show a man that you're different and not tell him how you got that way is not love. I've found that it's quite easy to gain an opportunity to share Christ with others, if you'll simply bridge the gap from deeds to words with a question, such as: "If you've got a few minutes, I'd like to share something with you that I think you'd find interesting. OK?" If they say no, just go on loving in deed and Christ will be glorified. If they say yes, you have an open door to share the real explanation for the abundance of your own life in Christ.

Remember too, that the purpose of God is not merely to get people saved and on their way to heaven. When your neighbor opens his heart to the truth of God, he has only begun and so have you. He receives new life, he is born—and you become a spiritual parent. Paul often spoke of those he saw added to the Lord as his own children (Galatians 4:19; 1 Thessalonians 2:11). He told the Corinthians that he became their father through the gospel (1 Corinthians 5:14-15). New Testament evangelism is parenthood and you're going to find yourself with a new baby on your hands! He'll have a thousand questions and a thousands needs. Many of these will be answered as he comes into the sharing body-ministry of the church. But you may find it very helpful to gather together once a week or so with just one or two of these new Christians at a time to study the Scriptures, pray together and just generally help them to get started on the right basis in the Christian life. This will take a lot of time, but that's what love does. And parenthood, natural or spiritual, is love more than anything else. Just think of the costly, time-consuming process that it takes to raise any child to maturity. It also holds true with our spiritual children. But remember that no normal parent resents that cost. Give yourself to these new believers and you'll see a church made up of men and women who have learned early to live by Christ, to minister to the believers, to teach their children and to love their neighbors.

> *It is not the main job of the church to turn out a lot of work, list a long string of members, or raise a lot of money. It is the main job of the church to fashion people who behave like Jesus Christ. They cannot be hewn out of the mediocre mass wholesale, but only one by one.*[1]

Another thing we need to be reminded of in this hour is that Jesus didn't send us out into the world just to repeat Scripture verses or to hand out tracts, but to go in the power of the Spirit to make men whole. "And as you go, proclaim, saying, 'The kingdom of heaven is at hand.' Heal the sick, raise the dead, cleanse the lepers, cast out demons; freely you received, freely give" (Matthew 10:7-8). "And they went out and preached everywhere while the Lord worked with them, and confirmed the word by the signs that followed" (Mark 16:20).

The need for many of us is simply to make ourselves available to God to be used in this "ministry of reconciliation." Many believers have become convinced that God can never use them in evangelism. They need to begin to expect God to do new things in their lives. For others of us, the need is to see evangelism in the balance of all that God is doing in this day, not as the ultimate purpose of God but as a very important step. All of us must see evangelism as the normal and spontaneous expression of the life of Jesus in every believer. Let the love of Christ control you to meet the needs of the lives around you each day.

May the Lord cause you to increase and abound in love for one another and for all men. . .so that He may establish your hearts unblameable (1 Thessalonians 3:12-13).

If. . .you are fulfilling the royal law, according to the Scripture, "You shall love your neighbor as yourself," you are doing well (James 2:8).

One of the chief accusations which I have heard leveled against body-fellowship groups is that they tend to become ingrown and unconcerned about the unbelievers around them. Sometimes, unfortunately, it is true. But this is usually where the emphasis is on the pattern rather than the life. Remember that just sitting in a circle or meeting in a home does not make a true expression of the body of Christ. His body has His life, and His life is concerned about the world, enough to give and give until that life is poured out for sinners.

New Testament fellowship has the potential to allow believers to develop spiritually so that they have life to share wherever they are. Where this is not the case, it won't help to go back to the "rah-rah pep rally" motivation. Instead, we need to see the lack of evangelism as a measure of the life in the group and let it cause us to turn to Christ so that more of what He is might be seen in us.

Early in the Acts "the Lord was adding to their number day by day." We are serving the same God today who loved the world enough to give His Son. And that love is not past. He still loves sinners and He is still giving His life for them, but now He's giving it through us. There are many Christians who believe that God is preparing His people and the world for one last great harvest of souls before the Day of the Lord. It may be. But I know this about the present: If you make yourself available to Christ, He'll make you available to people. And you'll see the life He has given you reproduced in others!

God demonstrates His own love toward us, in that while we were yet sinners, Christ died for us (Romans 5:8).

The love of God has been poured out within our hearts through the Holy Spirit who was given to us (Romans 5:5).

16

"SET APART. . .FOR THE WORK"

All through this book we have stressed the fact that all believers are in the "ministry," that this ministry is the spontaneous expression of the life of God in every believer, that the ministry of the local church is made up of all of those believers expressing life, and that there is no such thing as a special class of "ministers" or clergymen in the local church. But the question always comes, Who then were Paul, Barnabas, Silas, and others? Weren't they special workers of some kind, called to a particular ministry? The answer is a fast Yes, they were. They were special workers, called to a particular ministry. But this doesn't conflict with what I said earlier, because their special ministries were not in any way a part of the ministry of the local church. These men were apostles, and their entire work was something quite separate from the ministry of the local church. In fact, the very nature of their calling is that they were "set apart" from the local church and "sent out" to an itinerant and nonlocal ministry. The word *apostle* means "sent one."

Of course, many people in our day are convinced that the ministry or "office" of apostle no longer exists. Some people have ruled out apostles the same way they've ruled out the gifts of the Spirit for our day; they don't see any, and, therefore, they assume that they no longer exist. Others assume that the Bible only refers to the Twelve when it mentions apostles, and that when the Twelve died there were no more. But a closer look at the Word of God shows that neither of these assumptions is entirely correct.

In Ephesians, Paul tells us that God gave apostles to the church in the same sense that He gave prophets, evangelists, pastors and teachers (4:11). And in his first letter to the Corinthians, Paul says that God set in the church apostles, as well as other gifts ranging from teaching and helps to miracles and tongues (12:28). There is no more reason for thinking that we are not to have apostles today than there is for thinking that we are not to have teachers. Both are set in the church by God and are intended to continue in the work of equipping the saints for the ministry as long as the church remains on the earth.

There is no question but that the twelve apostles occupy a very special place both in the beginning of the church and for all eternity (see Revelation 21:14). But their special place and function don't prevent others from becoming "sent ones," or apostles, after them, any more than the fact that Jesus is referred to as "the Apostle" (Hebrews 3:1) would prevent the Twelve from being true apostles. Scripture shows us that Matthias was appointed to serve in the place of Judas (Acts 1:24-26) and that he was recognized by the Holy Spirit as one of the Twelve (Acts 6:2). But after his appointment, at least nine other men are mentioned by name as having served as apostles. The Lord's brother, James (Galatians 1:19), Barnabas, Paul (Acts 14:14), Andronicus, Junias (Romans 16:7), Apollos (1 Corinthians 4:6, 9), Epaphroditus (Philippians 2:25), Silvanus (Silas), and Timothy (1 Thessalonians 1:1, with 2:6) are all definitely called apostles in the New Testament, though in the case of some of these men the Greek word for apostles is incorrectly translated "messenger" in some English translations. In addition to these nine, Titus and the two brothers mentioned in 2 Corinthians 8:18, 22-23 might have been apostles as well. At any rate, we know that there were at least nine and possibly twelve apostles in the New Testament in addition to the Twelve. We also know that the "office" of apostle was intended by God to be a part of church life until the Lord's return.

If apostles are intended by God to be part of twentieth-century church life, where are they? Like many other elements of the New Testament church, the office of apostle was increasingly misunderstood, distorted, and finally laid aside by a rapidly declining church in the second and third centuries. Today God seems to be restoring many New Testament truths to His church. But the ironic truth is that while much of the weakness of today's church is due to the lack of true apostolic ministry, it is also true that we have few true apostles today because of the weakened state of the church. New Testament churches are the result of the ministry of New Testament apostles, but New Testament apostles are also the result of the ministry of New Testament churches. It's like the old analogy of the chicken and the egg—even if you can figure out which comes first, it's difficult to get started if you don't have either one. It does seem, however, that God is sovereignly beginning to raise up some local expressions of the body of Christ in our day which, it is hoped, will ultimately result in the preparation of more true sent ones. This would be in harmony with God's way of preparing apostles in the New Testament. Meanwhile, let's pray the Lord of the harvest to "send out laborers."

Life in the local church is the training ground for ministry of any kind. This is the principle we must keep in mind when we consider the preparation of an apostle. Don't make the common mistake of assuming that Paul became an apostle the day he saw a light on the road to Damascus. It was from ten to thirteen years later that he is first referred to as an apostle in the Acts and first begins to do the "work" of an apostle. This is the work God had originally chosen him for, but first there had to be years of preparation—years in which Paul was just a brother in the local church. During that time he was ministering, of course, but so was everyone else.

Since our generation has devised so many strange ways of preparing and training workers, let me share with you the simplicity of God's pattern as revealed in the New Testament. A man is first exposed to the gospel in the natural environment of his own daily life as some believer shares Christ with him. If there is a response in his heart to the good news, he is told that he must repent from dead works and put his faith in Christ. If he agrees, he is baptized into Christ and possibly hands might be laid upon him with prayer that he might be clothed with the power of the Spirit for ministry. Then he is introduced into the fellowship of the local church where he is taught the meaning of what has happened to him (Hebrews 6:1). Basically he is taught that he has received the life of Christ and that Christ's life in him will express itself as ministry. As this new brother fellowships with the local church, it becomes apparent to him and to the other believers just what his ministry or ministries are in the body. This is not just a matter of self-discovery since the principle of the body is submission to one another. If his ministry is genuinely of the Spirit, it will soon become apparent to everyone. As he continues fellowshiping with the church, he exercises his ministry, expressing life every day with both believers and unbelievers. Exercise strengthens, and he becomes increasingly more fruitful. But he's also learning a great deal more than just the improvement of his own ministry.

This amazing atmosphere of the body of Christ is made possible as each believer looks to Christ as the head, and as each one voluntarily places himself in subjection to the others (Ephesians 5:21), considering others as more important than himself (Philippians 2:3). In this atmosphere this new Christian begins to learn about others' ministries as well, gaining a rich and varied experience of body-life. By his submission to the others, he is continually checked as to whether he is in the Spirit himself or not. Thus he learns by experience what it means to walk consistently in the Spirit. But even more important than this, if he is to continue successfully in fellowship, he will have to experience a deep work of the cross—a real crucifixion of the self-life. He will be in constant fellowship with brothers and sisters who are individuals too, who think and do things differently, who make mistakes, who are not always in the Spirit, and who are sometimes downright unkind and cruel to him. Unless he is willing to die to self, to bear the cross daily, he cannot survive in church life. And unless he survives in church life he can never become an apostle.

It is absolutely imperative that an apostle be one who has learned in depth, not only to recognize and exercise fruitfully his own gifts of ministry, but to know the operation of others' ministries as well. But beyond that, he must have learned in depth to be consistent in his walk in the Spirit. And even beyond that, he must have thoroughly died to self so that the self-life doesn't get in the way in carrying out the work of an apostle. And there is no place in the world to learn these things like a local church which fellowships on the basis of a functioning expression of the body of Christ. This is why the training ground for apostles is the fellowship of the church.

I suppose it would be possible to learn some of these things to a lesser degree apart from the body. But not in the measure that God requires to qualify a man for the spiritually exacting work of planting churches. Today men have created various schools and seminaries for the purpose of training workers. In these institutions men can learn facts about the Bible, and may even experience something of the cross in an individual way. But a classroom in a school will never come close to experience in the local church.

Another thing we are observing today is the tendency of men who have had some training and experience as leaders in the organized church to assume that they are apostles when they first learn a little about the New Testament church pattern. It seems so very difficult for these men to come down from their exalted position once they have been "up there." Yet this very difficulty and hesitancy shows how desperately they need to just "drop it," let their "ministries" go into death, so that in the atmosphere of the local church God can bring about a resurrection by the power of the Spirit.

There are now a good many such men running about the country "ministering" to church-in-the-home groups. But I suggest that you be very slow to accept the ministry of someone who has not spent time as a brother in a local church in submission to the body of Christ. These self-appointed "apostles" often tend to carry much of the "old school" institutionalism over into the new thing God is doing, and I have seen some of them wreak havoc by their soulish, immature ministries. For how can a man appoint elders unless he has been one himself? How can he advise the church on discipline or on the exercise of the gifts unless he has personally experienced such situations himself? How can he even know and recognize what his ministry in the Spirit is unless it has been recognized and confirmed by the brothers who know him well? And how can he be totally submitted to God and to his fellow apostles unless he has learned repeatedly to regard others as genuinely more important than himself in church life?

God's pattern is to keep a man within the ranks of local church ministry until he has prepared a man who is thoroughly trustworthy, who can be depended upon to express the life of Christ consistently and to reproduce that life in others. Then God speaks by His Spirit, "Set apart for me Barnabas and Saul for the work to which I have called them" (Acts 13:2). And when He speaks, He speaks not only to the one being set apart, but to the church as well. There is absolutely no ground for a brother to leave the local church for "the work" without the unanimous confirmation by the Spirit to the church. To leave without the confirmation of the church is almost certainly to leave before the preparation is completed.

> *Then, when they had fasted and prayed and laid their hands on them, they let them go. So, being sent out by the Holy Spirit, they went. . .(Acts 13:3-4, free translation).*

Notice that it is the Holy Spirit who sends them out, but it is the church that let them go. Since this is a very serious matter, it is done with much prayer and fasting. It has taken a long time to prepare these men and there is no hurry to let them go out.

After the Holy Spirit has been obeyed, the "sent-ones" are "set apart for the work." What are they set apart from? They are set apart from the local church. There are no apostles in the local church. The basic characteristic of an apostle is that he is sent out—set apart from the local situation for a ministry as wide and as vast as the universal body of Christ. As he goes out he has no structured organizational (or financial) relationship to the local church which let him go. As an apostle, he is basically itinerant—"separated unto the work."

As God sends him out into the work, there are indications that he is an apostle: his Christ-like character, his maturity, his proven ministry, and the confirmation of his home church. There are also two other indications: "The signs of a true apostle were performed among you with all perserverance, by signs and wonders and miracles" (2 Corinthians 12:12). We have already mentioned God's promise to confirm His Word with signs and wonders through all His church, using even the least of His children in this way at times. Surely, then, these things ought to be part of the ministry of a true apostle. Paul seems to indicate here that if these evidences of God's power were not apparent in a man's ministry, there would be room for considerable doubt regarding his apostleship.

Of the sufferings of an apostle, Paul has even more to say: "God has exhibited us apostles last of all, as men condemned to death; because we have become a spectacle to the world, both to angels and to men. . . .To this present hour we are both hungry and thirsty, and are poorly clothed, and are roughly treated, and are homeless; and we toil, working with our own hands; when we are reviled, we bless; when we are persecuted, we endure; when we are slandered, we try to conciliate; we have become as the scum of the world, the dregs of all things, even until now" (1 Corinthians 4:9-13).

In his second letter to the Corinthians, Paul goes into even greater detail, mentioning the terrible beatings he had received, the dangers of travel, the cost of constant battle with false teachers, plus many other types of spiritual, emotional, and physical hardships (6:4-10; 11:23-28). But all of this was viewed by Paul as part of the apostle's life. "Now I rejoice in my sufferings for your sake, and in my flesh I do my share on behalf of His body (which is the church) in filling up that which is lacking in Christ's afflictions" (Colossians 1:24). Any man who is truly set apart for the work of God cannot expect to avoid the sufferings of Christ.

The "work" basically consists of two things. One is to evangelize and to plant new churches. The other is to build up the existing churches so that they will become better expressions of the body of Christ. To do this, the apostle will need to hold meetings with the Christians of the area. If he is to be in the area for any length of time these meetings should be separate and distinct from the regular meetings of the church in that area. This is where the difference between the church and the work becomes very practical. The meetings of the work are for the purpose of allowing one man to instruct a group of others and would usually take a form similar to a preaching service in the organized church. The apostle would teach and answer questions while the others remain relatively passive. Of course, this is totally unlike the usual meetings of the church where each one shares what God has given him. If the apostle were only visiting the church a few days and he were to dominate the meeting with his teaching, no great harm would be done, but if he remains for a longer period of time and replaces the meetings of the church with his own teaching meetings, there will be a great tendency for the church to lose sight of its calling to function as a body and it may end with the apostle settling down to become the "pastor" of the local church. This would hinder both the work and the church.

The accompanying diagram shows the distinctiveness of the work and the local church. The apostle teaches the Christians the "elementary teaching" about Christ and His church. He also instructs the people to begin to meet in their own homes for fellowship as a church. While he is there, the people will attend both kinds of meetings. But when he leaves, the fellowship of the church continues. Eventually this fellowship will result in the training of more workers, who will plant more churches. If the Spirit is allowed to lead, a beautiful balance will result with both the work and the local church prospering. But always remember that the work is only temporarily a part of the local picture until the apostle moves on, whereas the local church will always express Christ in that area as long as there are two or three to gather in His name.

The Universal Body of Christ

THE WORK	THE LOCAL CHURCH
APOSTLES – "SENT ONES"	ELDERS
1. Nonlocal—itinerant	1. All local
2. Evangelize	2. Plural
3. Plant churches	3. Not paid money
4. Build up churches	4. Pastoral
5. Live by faith	
	DEACONS
	1. Local
	2. Oversee material needs

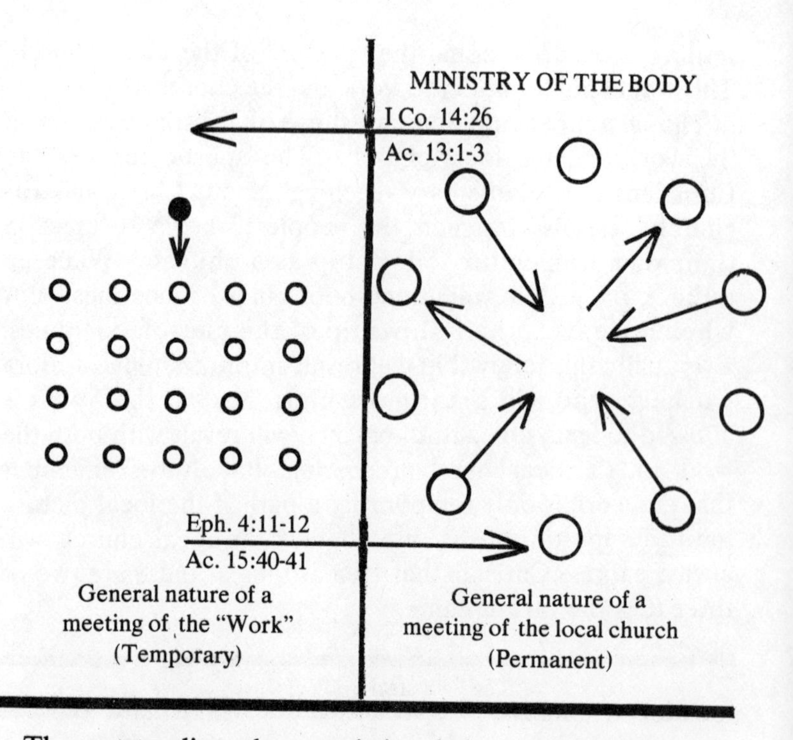

The outstanding characteristic of the apostles' finances was *faith* of the purest kind. And faith is depending upon God and not on anyone or anything else. That's why you will never find any of the first-century apostles making any appeal for funds, taking any offerings, or making their needs known in any way. Paul, of course, did make appeals for collections to aid other Christians who were in great need (1 Corinthians 16:1; 2 Corinthians 8-10), but he never asks or even hints that this should be done for himself. Nor does he ever talk about being in need in such a way as to subtly influence the churches into sending him a gift. He made his needs known only to God. This gave God the control of the work at a most practical point. Paul expected God to speak to the churches because he had confidence that each believer was able to be led by the Spirit directly.

Part of the time Paul's needs were met as he worked hard

at his tent-making occupation (Acts 18:3; 1 Corinthians 4:12). He often provided for his fellow workers this way too (Acts 20:33-34). If a gift came from some far away church, Paul thanked them and praised God for it (2 Corinthians 11:9; Philippians 4:10). But whether it did or not, the work was not affected. Paul also had a firm rule that he would never take gifts or offerings from the church where he was presently ministering (2 Corinthians 11:8-9; 1 Thessalonians 2:9; 2 Thessalonians 3:7-8). To do this might give some the opportunity to say that he was only there for the money. He never had or sought pledged regular support from anyone or any church. Nor did he ever suggest that any of the churches were under any sort of obligation to support him, even though many of them owed their very existence to his ministry. Watchman Nee makes a good point when he says that a man who cannot trust God completely in the area of finances lacks the first qualification for the work.[1]

The attitude of Christian workers to financial matters will be a fairly good indication as to whether or not they have been commissioned of God. If the work is of God it will be spiritual, and if the work is spiritual the way of supply will be spiritual. If supplies are not on a spiritual plane, then the work itself will speedily drift on to the plane of secular business.

If a man can trust God, let him go and work for Him. If not, let him stay at home, for he lacks the first qualification for the work. There is an idea prevalent that if a worker has a settled income he can be more at leisure for the work and consequently will do it better, but as a matter of fact, in spiritual work there is a need for an unsettled income, because that necessitates intimate fellowship with God, constant clear revelation of His will, and direct divine support. In worldly business all a worker needs by way of equipment is will and talent, but human zeal and natural gift are no equipment for spiritual service. Utter dependence upon God is necessary if the work is to be according to His will; therefore God wishes His workers to be cast on Him alone for their financial supplies, so that they cannot but walk in close communion with Him and learn to trust Him continually. The more an attitude of trustful dependence on God is cultivated, the more spiritual the work will be. So it is clear that the nature of the work and the source of its supply are closely related.[2]

It's hard to grasp in this day of ecclesiastical and institutional churches, but the relationship between Paul and the churches was a spiritual one, not an organizational one. Once the elders were appointed and the church set in order, the apostle had no authority in the local church organizationally. He did have a spiritual responsibility which he met as a father. And the churches had no organizational ties with him. They had a spiritual responsibility, which they exercised with prayer and occasional gifts. (See chapter 17.) But even when they didn't, the work went on, for it was only dependent upon God, and upon Paul's relationship to Him.

The apostles frequently traveled in bands. This was not just because it took several men to get the work done. The principle of body-fellowship and submission to the brothers carried over into the work and the daily spiritual needs of the apostles were often met by one another. But again, their relationship was a spiritual one and not organizational. They did not organize together as "missions" or organizations. If they had done so, they would have almost certainly ended up promoting and reproducing the organization rather than local, autonomous churches. The purpose of the work is to plant churches in the name of the Lord and not to establish local branches or chapters of an organization, nor to extend the borders of a denomination. A band of apostles worked together as long as the Spirit led them to do so, planting churches and edifying the existing churches. Later they went their separate ways and the churches they had planted belonged to the Lord and not to them or their organization. Afterward, another band of workers might come along and help the same churches on toward greater maturity.

I think you can see that it takes a man with a total disregard for his own pride, position, desires, security, and even his own life to carry out the work as God intended. This is a man who has learned truly to deny himself and lose his own life. It also takes a man who is thoroughly prepared by the Spirit in every phase of ministry and church life. And most of all it takes a man who is a constant expression of the life of Christ—so much so that he can say to the churches, "Be imitators of me" (1 Corinthians 11:1), and not risk a perversion of the purpose of God. I don't think there are many such men around today. But I do think that God is at work preparing some. In some of these feeble little house-churches God has men in whom He is working. It may take some time, because this is a process that can't be hurried. But it will help if you and I are praying for them. And the key is that each of us continue faithfully in fellowship, making ourselves available to God without presuming to be anything that God has not specifically made evident. If each of us seeks only to express His life and find our own part in the body, God will do the rest and workers will be prepared.

For through the grace given to me I say to every man among you not to think more highly of himself than he ought to think (Romans 12:3).

17

THE BATTLE WITH MAMMOM

The question of finance has most important issues. In grace God is the greatest power, but in the world mammon is the greatest. If God's servants do not clearly settle the question of finance, then they leave a vast number of other questions unsettled too. Once the financial problem is solved, it is amazing how many other problems are automatically solved with it too.[1]

As Watchman Nee suggests in the quote above, there are not many things that offer as much opportunity for carnal problems as does money in the church. Also there are few areas in which we have as many incredibly bad examples surrounding us in contemporary experience. It was a serious enough problem in the days of Paul, but today we've found so many clever ways of doing it worse and making it look better. If the local church and the workers who are sent out are going to be reflections of the Lord's life, there must be a very significant return to New Testament teaching in this matter.

By now I'm sure you realize that the underlying principle of the New Testament teaching on any matter is a liberal dose and display of the love of God through His people. Even more so when it comes to finances. "Do not merely look out for your own personal interests, but also for the interests of others" (Philippians 2:4) is a principle which is applied again and again in the Scriptures to the handling of money. Love is the solution. But love is never abstract, as we've seen in some other areas. Its appearance can always be described, and the New Testament record of how finances were handled is one of the best descriptions of love that you will find.

We've already seen the attitude of New Testament workers toward financial matters. They simply lived in such a way as not to be dependent upon anyone or anything but God. But some of the Christians were sensitive to the needs of the workers and were directed by the Spirit of God to send gifts to them. They did this even though there was no organizational responsibility; the apostles had never requested such help, and the Christians knew that the custom of the workers was to sometimes make their own way. The Philippians were especially commended by Paul for this.

> *But I rejoiced in the Lord greatly, that now at last you have revived your concern for me; indeed, you were concerned before, but you lacked opportunity.*
>
> *Not that I speak from want; for I have learned to be content in whatever circumstances I am. I know how to get along with humble means, and I also know how to live in prosperity; in any and every circumstance I have learned the secret of being filled and going hungry, both of having abundance and suffering need. I can do all things through Him who strengthens me.*
>
> *Nevertheless, you have done well to share with me in my affliction. And you yourselves also know, Philippians, that at the first preaching of the gospel, after I departed from Macedonia, no church shared with me in the matter of giving and receiving but you alone; for even in Thessalonica you sent a gift more than once for my needs. Not that I seek the gift itself, but I seek for the profit which increases to your account. But I have received everything in full, and have an abundance; I am amply supplied, having received from Epaphroditus what you have sent, a fragrant offering, an acceptable sacrifice, well pleasing to God (Philippians 4:10-18).*

Notice that while Paul commends them highly and even says that their act of giving has great value in the sight of

God, he also goes out of his way to state that he now has no need at all and that it wouldn't matter if he did, rather than saying something that would entice them to give again. In this is the key. Workers must work as though independent of financial help from the churches, but the churches do have a spiritual responsibility and will be honoring God by helping the workers financially. The important thing is that the stimulus for giving come from God and not from the workers. Giving to workers should be solely on the basis of the direction of the Spirit, for the Spirit knows far better than we what the need is and how it should be met. Christians should never be guided by appeals, "prayer" letters, promotions, or needs made obvious by the workers.

Wouldn't it be interesting if, beginning today, all stewardship in Christendom were placed exclusively on the basis of the leading of the Spirit and all workers who made appeals of any kind were excluded? I don't suppose it's likely to happen, since Christendom is organized on such a soulish basis, but it's surely worth a try. I do know that you yourself will profit by looking to the Spirit for direction in giving because it is sure to increase your sensitivity to the Spirit in other things as well. The workers who really live by faith will not be hurt and the others could use a good lesson in spiritual economics.

The other aspect of New Testament giving was for the relief of fellow Christians. This ranged all the way from inviting the neighbors over for supper to the situation in Acts 4 where they sold houses and lands and shared the proceeds. "Not one of them claimed that anything belonging to him was his own; but that all things were common property to them" (Acts 4:32).

The basis of this kind of giving, and the giving to workers as well, was need together with the direction of the Spirit, not the Old Testament tithe. The tithe was a legalistic guide for giving by the people before God's Spirit was poured out on all flesh. Its purpose was to support an ecclesiastical system of priests which is made totally unnecessary by the priesthood of all believers in the New Testament. The tithe is never mentioned in the New Testament except to refer to the Old Testament practice. God's church has no temples and no hired priests to support, and God's workers live by the mercy of God like the Old Testament prophets, not like the priests. So tithing is not the principle for stewardship in the church, though it may suggest a point at which to begin. But we are responsible to the Lord for all we possess, not for a mere 10 percent.

Let me say it again: the basis of giving for the relief of Christians was the need and the need was met as the Spirit led. In the early days in Jerusalem, thousands were suddenly converted to faith in a Christ who had been crucified in that same city only a short time earlier (Acts 2:41; 4:4). No doubt many of these lost jobs, homes, and families for the faith. Hundreds of others were probably only visitors in the city who had come for the Jewish feasts and had responded to the message of the Christians (Acts 2:5-10). Probably many stayed on in the city for fellowship and the teaching of the apostles rather than returning home as originally planned. All of these dispossessed and out-of-towners had to be provided for. So, when the need was great, the response was great. These people lived by the life of Christ within them and as God directed them, they sold what they owned to help the others.

Common property was not the general custom in the churches later in the New Testament, not because the first effort failed (as some have supposed), but because the need was not that great again in most cases. Today there is an increasing tendency for groups of Christians to live communally, holding all things in common. When it is done by the leading of the Spirit and in an atmosphere of real love, it can provide a powerful testimony in the midst of this incredibly materialistic generation. One outstanding illustration is the Reba Place fellowship in Evanston, Illinois.

Here fifteen or more families live, pooling their incomes, and living in homes owned by the group. Excess funds are used to aid other Christians, for the poor, or for such other purposes as may be decided by the fellowship. Since all the families live within a one-or two-block radius, there is a wonderful atmosphere of constant fellowship and ministry.

There are variations of this. Placing the fellowship of the believers as a priority above material things has led several members of our group to relocate their homes nearer to one another. In some groups, single members have been taken into the homes of families in the group. We find an increasing tendency to share with one another as we find that someone is going to have a baby, someone else is moving or remodeling, and so forth. I know of other instances where there are two families sharing a home, or where several Christian families have banded together to buy an apartment building which they occupy together. Even though community property is not demanded by the example of the New Testament church, it's a healthy thing where there is a growing attitude of "all things in common" among believers, even though it may not be actual communal living.

The early Christians did continue to meet the needs of their brothers and sisters. The mass need continued for several years in Jerusalem, partly because of a famine (Acts 11:27-30) and possibly also because of the continuing persecution of the believers there (Acts 8:1-4). Several contributions were sent there from time to time by both individuals and various churches. But in every community there were some Christians who were poor, dispossessed, widowed, orphaned, in want. Their needs, in that day of no insurance or social security, had to be met by other Christians or they would not be met at all. Still the basis was the need, the resources of the giver, and the prompting of the Spirit to the heart of each man.

And in the proportion that any of the disciples had means, each of them determined to send a contribution for the relief of the brethren living in Judea (Acts 11:29).

Let each one do just as he has purposed in his heart; not grudgingly or under compulsion; for God loves a cheerful giver. And God is able to make all grace abound to you, that always having all sufficiency in everything, you may have an abundance for every good deed (2 Corinthians 9:7-8).

When the needs of local Christians became large and widespread enough that it began to take time and care to distribute what was given to them, the church would appoint deacons to handle this task (Acts 6:1-6). As deacons, they had the oversight of these material needs and would disperse, not control, the funds for this purpose under the direction of the church. But don't get the idea that all these men did was to carry the purse. They were Spirit-filled men of proven fruitfulness and wisdom in other ministries, and the example of Philip and Stephen shows that these fruitful ministries both continued and increased after they were appointed deacons. Paul told Timothy that the primary qualification of a deacon was that he must be a man who is "holding fast to the mystery of the faith with a clear conscience" (1 Timothy 3:9). In other words, he had to be a man who was living by faith in the indwelling Christ, who is the mystery of godliness. His office was deacon, but his ministry could be any expression of the life of Christ in addition to his work as a deacon.

People being what they are, there was a tendency for some to try to take advantage of the compassion of the Christians. It was necessary for the churches to make sure that they weren't taking in "meal-ticket Christians." Consequently, Paul told Timothy that widows should be supported by their own grown children or grandchildren if at all possible. The younger widows were to get busy and remarry. If they were supported by the church they would not have enough to do and would only get into trouble. Even the older widows were supported only if they were real prayer warriors and were known for their godly works (1 Timothy 5:3-16). The purpose of helping the poor was not to make them idle.

With men, the rule was, "If anyone will not work, neither let him eat" (2 Thessalonians 3:10). "Work with your hands, just as we commanded you; so that you may behave properly toward outsiders and not be in any need" (1 Thessalonians 4:11-12). Paul also said that a man who does not provide for his family "has denied the faith, and is worse than an unbeliever" (1 Timothy 5:8). Strong words! Yet we need to see that all of these warnings were only the outside borders of a tremendous compassion which caused the church to continually meet the needs of every believer who was genuinely in need and either temporarily or permanently unable to help themselves.

Now as to the love of the brethren, you have no need for anyone to write to you, for you yourselves are taught by God to love one another (1 Thessalonians 4:9).

What use is it, my brethren, if a man says he has faith, but he has no works? Can that faith save him? If a brother or sister is without clothing and in need of daily food, and one of you says to them, "Go in peace, be warmed and filled"; and yet you do not give them what is necessary for their body what use is that? Even so faith, if it has no deeds, is dead, being by itself (James 2:14-17).

Even though we live in the day of social security, welfare programs, and insurance for life, health and income, our cities are still filled with Christians in desperate need. And from time to time, in almost every fellowship there will be occasions of need that spring up which only the love of God in the believers can meet. "Let each of you do just as he has purposed in his own heart" (2 Corinthians 9:7).

There is one other item of finance that might come up in the local church. From time to time, a brother or brothers might be led by the Spirit into some special project such as literature publishing, a coffee house, an orphanage, a rehabilitation house for drug addicts. Regardless of how needy these special efforts may become, it's important that the

Christian or Christians to whom God gave the vision be responsible before God for the financing of them. This means that the burden should not be placed on the church and that precisely the same principles of faith should apply to these efforts as apply to the support of the workers. The one who starts such an effort should be personally responsible to look to God for all the needs, including the salaries of any helpers necessary to carry out secular aspects of the effort.

As I said at the beginning of this chapter, money can be the occasion for all sorts of carnal behavior. But it can also be the opportunity for some really extraordinary displays of the love of God as the Christian, filled with the life of Christ, moves directly cross-grain from the materialistic society and the influence of the prince of this world. "Let love be without hypocrisy" (Romans 12:9).

> *But whoever has the world's goods, and beholds his brother in need and closes his heart against him, how does the love of God abide in him? Little children, let us not love with word or with tongue, but in deed and truth. We shall know by this that we are of the truth, and shall assure our heart before him (1 John 3:17-19).*

18

DILIGENT TO PRESERVE THE UNITY

Make my joy complete by being of the same mind, maintaining the same love, united in spirit, intent on one purpose (Philippians 2:2).

We've already seen that the basic purpose of the church is to be an expression of the nature and attributes of God in this world. Since God is love, it follows that Jesus would say, "By this will all men know that you are My disciples, if you have love for one another" (John 13:35). And later He prayed for the church, "That they may all be one; even as Thou, Father, art in Me, and I in Thee, that they also may be in Us; that the world may believe that Thou didst send Me" (John 17:21). If the world is to believe our words about Christ, they must see a demonstration of His love expressed through unity in the church.

"Has Christ been divided?" (1 Corinthians 1:13). Paul's question has been repeated again and again down through the centuries by the world about us as they have seen the sectarianism which divides and redivides the body of Christ. We seem to be saying with our words that the death and resurrection of Jesus are not sufficient to reconcile us to one while with our actions we are saying that the death and reusrrection of Jesus are not sufficient to reconcile us to one another. Under the circumstances, who can blame the world for not believing?

I doubt that there has ever been a generation which needed a demonstration of the unity of God's people more than this one. But we're not likely to see it until we rediscover what the true basis of scriptural unity really is. Many sincere efforts at uniting God's people today will fail because they lack the scriptural basis. The effort which captures most of the headlines, of course, is the ecumenical movement, an attempt to join all of the major denominations organizationally into one world church. The Scriptures plainly indicate that the ultimate end of this will be a false world-church. Soulish organization can never bring about or be the basis for true Christian unity. On the other hand there are those who cling to the thought that one day everyone will wake up and discover the "true doctrine" (their own, of course) and then we will be able to unite in "the truth." Not only does it seem unlikely, but that kind of unity too would be based on a false premise. Neither doctrine nor organization forms the basis of unity among believers. There are some efforts which fit into a third category. These seek to temporarily set aside doctrinal differences, minimize organization, and unite for the sake of the work to be done, usually the work of evangelism. This is much closer than the first two, but it still lacks a full grasp of the oneness of the New Testament church.

New Testament Christians were one in Christ! And that's the simplicity of it. Their unity was not in Christ's teachings and doctrines, not in His organization, and not even in His work. They were simply one in Him! To be a Christian in essence is to have your human spirit joined to His Holy Spirit. This means that you are one spirit with Him—you are in Christ. Now, if you are one spirit with Him and I am one spirit with Him—if you are in Christ and I am in Christ—then we are one in Christ! And that fact alone forms the basis of our fellowship and our unity with others.

Wherefore, accept one another, just as Christ also accepted us to the glory of God (Romans 15:7).

On what basis did Christ accept you? Was it because you were doctrinally all straightened out? Was it because you were ready to "join" the right organization? Was it because you were ready to didicate your life to the fulfillment of the Great Commission? Or was it even because you had so changed that there was no element of sin, failure, or weakness left in your behavior? No, it was none of these things. It was on the basis of grace that you were accepted by Him. You weren't much, but He accepted you. And I'm not much either, but you must accept me. And the basis will simply be my testimony that Christ dwells within—that's all! (Unless, of course, the nature of my life proves to be a denial of that testimony.)

This is the true basis for all Christian unity. I have a personal relationship to Christ and you have a personal relationship to Christ; therefore we have a relationship to one another. But suppose that I don't have the doctrinal light that you have, or suppose that I don't measure up to your standards of behavior? (We are not speaking of immoral persons or of those who teach destructive doctrines warned against in Scripture.) Or maybe I insist on things that you know are really not necessary, but only result from my weakness? "Now accept the one who is weak in faith, but not for the purpose of passing judgement on his opinions" (Romans 14:1). The word is still the same: *accept* one another just as Christ also accepted us. If Christ accepts me but you don't, you have put yourself above Christ. That has got to be wrong!

The New Testament believers simply accepted this basis of unity without question. That's why, in the New Testament, no name is ever given to a church other than the name of the city in which the church met. There is the church of Ephesus, the church at Antioch, and so forth. But there is no church of the such-and-such doctrine or of the so-and-so method. The basis of fellowship was the Lord, and the church in Ephesus was simply all the people in Ephesus who enjoyed an inner spiritual relationship with Him. They didn't all meet in one place, but neither were they divided by sectarianism, doctrine, organization, or emphasis. And whenever this kind of division arose, it was soundly denounced.

In the Corinthian church, there was much doctrinal confusion, some even denying the resurrection of the Lord. There was gross misunderstanding and misuse of the gifts of the Spirit. People were coming together for the Lord's Supper and getting drunk. Paul rebuked all of these, but the only man he suggested they actually disfellowship was one who was living in open immorality and who refused to give it up. But most of all, Paul was concerned about their unity. He was firm that there should be no division in the body, and even suggested that those who persist in dividing the body are guilty of destroying the temple of God, which is the church (1 Corinthians 1:12; 3:4, 16-67).

All of this is not to suggest that doctrine is not important (see Titus 1:1—2:15), or that we should not be genuinely concerned about various aspects of Christian behavior. I have suggested in this book some basic beliefs which I and others hold to quite firmly. Scripture says, "Let each man be fully convinced in his own mind" (Romans 14:5). But none of these things can be made the *basis of fellowship* if we are to be true to the Scriptures. Our fellowship is in Him and in Him alone! And we must always be careful that we are open to fellowship with all those who have fellowship with Him.

This unity we are talking about is, in one sense, an accomplished fact. This is what is sometimes called the "mystical union" of the church. But there is another sense in which it needs to be expressed to be real. And that expression, to make the impact on the world which God is seeking, must be practical and it must be where you are—in the local church.

The most basic, and at times the most difficult, expression of oneness in Christ must take place between believers within the local church. This is at the heart of what it means to fellowship as a body, and each of the major references to the body ministry in the New Testament is accompanied with an emphasis on being one in Christ. The epistles to the churches are filled with exhortations along this line too. The one that means the most to me is in Philippians 2:2-4.

Make my joy complete by being of the same mind, maintaining the same love, united in spirit, intent on one purpose. Do nothing from selfishness or empty conceit, but with humility of mind let each of you regard one another as more important than himself; do not merely look out for your own personal interests, but also for the interests of others.

Paul follows this by referring to the perfect example of Jesus, who set aside His divine rights for us and ended on the cross. And this is what it takes to have unity in the church —the cross. This means we cannot insist on our own way. Our constant attitude must be to look out for the good of the other, even if it means suffering and even if he refuses to look out for our good.

One of the greatest chapters about the church in the Bible is Ephesians 4. In this chapter, Paul explains the granting of spiritual gifts, the ministry of the believers, and the operation of the body. But he begins and ends the chapter with a plea for a willingness to suffer so that unity might prevail.

I. . .intreat you to walk in a manner worthy of the calling with which you have been called, with all humility and gentleness, with patience, showing forbearance to one another in love, being diligent to preserve the unity of the Spirit in the bond of peace. There is one body, and one Spirit (Ephesians 4:1-4).

Let all bitterness and wrath and anger and clamor and slander be put away from you, along with all malice. And be kind to one another, tender-hearted, forgiving one another, just as God in Christ also has forgiven you (Ephesians 4:31-32).

In any group of Christians who gather together for fellowship there will be variety. There will be variety in background, doctrine, temperament, gifts, manner of worship, and many other things. We know that not all variety is of the Spirit; some is just an expression of the flesh. But the answer is not to see unity through uniformity or conformity.

We will never have everyone in the church alike but we already have them in Christ. In Him we are one. Let's continually ask the Spirit to create within us a mind to express that oneness with the church. This attitude of selflessness will be present in the church if each individual takes care to live by the indwelling life of Christ, for this is the way His life behaves. Oneness between individuals in the church despite natural differences will bring much glory to God.

UNITY IN DECISIONS

There is another way in which unity needs to be expressed in the local church. This is the matter of unity when the church must take corporate action on something. Since the church represents God in the world, it is vitally important to be sure that all its courses of action are pleasing to Him. Christ must be the literal head of the church. This cannot be brought about by a democratic vote or by the rule of the elders. The mind of the Lord must be found in the undivided conviction of the entire local body.

The democratic vote is probably one of the most reasonable methods for natural men to find the opinion of the majority, or even to find the "best" way. But the church is not intended to express either the opinion of the majority or the "best" way. It is intended to express the mind of the Lord in any given matter.

In John 17:20-13, Jesus prayed that we as Christians would be an expression of the oneness of the Godhead. They act as one because They are one: one spirit, one mind, and always one course of action.

I know that some will protest that it is simply impossible to get complete agreement in a group of any size. But remember that the things which are impossible with men are possible with God, and the church is out to demonstrate that fact. "The multitude of those who believed were of one heart and soul. . . ." (Acts 4:32). ". . .day by day continuing with one mind. . ." (Acts 2:46).

Let's come back to the basics. The local church is a group of people, each of whom is personally indwelt by the Spirit of God. He is there to direct and control their lives so that each individually and all corporately are an expression of His life. If He is not present in their lives, there is no church. If He is not able to speak to open and yielded hearts, He is not God. But if He is there and if He is able, then there is no reason that each decision should not wait until He has revealed His will to every individual by the Spirit. If a group is not able to come to that unity, then there is a spiritual problem which will certainly not be resolved by going ahead on the opinion of the majority.

There are three levels of decision-making which will occur in the believer's life from time to time. The first is that of personal decisions involving home, family, job, finances, and other personal matters. These are not decisions to be made by the church but by the individual as he looks to the Lord for direction. Any of these areas might become the business of his fellow Christians if it seemed that he were being led into sin, but normally these decisions would be his to make as an individual.

The second level is that of ministry. We minister as part of the body of Christ, not as individuals, and I have already mentioned that God uses those in the body to serve as checks upon one another as to whether or not they be of the Spirit. For these reasons, decision-making on the level of ministry is a matter of church concern as well as individual. By this I don't mean that anyone should sit back and expect the others to find the will of God for his life for him, or to decide the nature of his ministry. But as God moves him to various types of ministry, he should be sharing this with the others and looking for real confirmation in the Spirit. In the final analysis each one must receive his direction from the Lord and the decision will also be individual. But ignoring the counsel of spiritual brothers is a risky course.

The third level is that of decisions which must be made

regarding actions which will be taken by the local church corporately. I think it almost goes without saying that these kinds of decisions must be made only as God's will is made clear through unanimity in His people.

Let's arrange the elements of such a situation into the proper priorities. The most important thing is that we be truly one in Him and that the mind of the Lord be expressed. Second in importance is that every individual in the church be sensitive enough to the Spirit of God to be individually led by Him. These first two go hand-in-hand. Last in importance is the urgency of the actual decision facing the church. Because of these priorities, no decision is so urgent that it cannot wait until every individual has found the mind of the Lord in the matter and until all are in agreement as to what His mind is in the matter. The devil is always in a hurry—his time is running out—but the Lord has eternity. Frequently, if it seems that a decision must be made without sufficient time for each one to find the mind of the Lord, you will eventually discover that the urgency was a trick of the enemy to rush the church into losing its oneness in Christ. His nature is to divide; God's nature is to reconcile. Our primary concern should be, "Thy will be done, on earth as it is in heaven" (Matthew 6:10).

At least one other expression of unity is needed. This is the matter of unity in the community between various groups who gather regularly for fellowship. The biggest key here will be to constantly remember that fellowship is not on a basis of doctrine. We ourselves must never gather on sectarian grounds and, even though others might, we must not refuse to fellowship with them because they do. It's probably not physically possible to meet with all the believers in your community, but be careful to keep the lines of communication open. Be ready to share the Lord's life with one another when you do meet, rather than discussing the areas which you see differently.

This also means that no group must claim to be "the"

church of their area by inferring in any way that others are not. It may be that they do not understand the principle of body-fellowship, they gather on sectarian grounds, they disagree with you on doctrine, and they even refuse to fellowship with you. Still, if they are people in whom Christ dwells, they must be regarded as brothers and sisters in the Lord and as part of the local church in your community. It will help to express this kind of oneness if you avoid naming your church or fellowship group. And in some cases, it will be better if you meet at a time other than the other groups in the area, leaving more opportunity for fellowship.

Fundamental to all of this is the fact that all true unity among believers is on the basis of our sharing one Spirit. We cannot call unclean what God has cleansed and we must accept one another as Christ has accepted us. We must forgive one another as Christ has forgiven us. There may be those with whom we cannot colabor, as our understanding of evangelism or church planting, for instance, may be very different from theirs. But we must always remain open to fellowship on the basis of sharing Him and His life with one another. Every man must be fully convinced in his own mind as to the purpose and ways of God, but his convictions must not be used to judge others and to cut them off from any fellowship they may desire.

IT LOOKS LIKE LOVE

The burden of this book has been to say that the church, if it is to be anything worthwhile, is to be an expression of the life of God dwelling within the spirits of His people. And God is love. When His life is expressed it always looks like love. If it looks like something else, it probably is something else—another kind of life, perhaps satanic, perhaps only human. Neither of these will do. God's eternal purpose for man is that he be an expression of the highest life in the universe, the original, uncreated life of God, who is love.

I have tried to show in this book that there is a great deal of detailed information about the Christian life and about the church in the Scriptures that has been frequently overlooked. These details are not unimportant. If we are faithful to live by His life, they will become part of our daily living and our fellowship. We are very fortunate to live in a day when God is restoring so much truth to His church. But always we must remember the essence of it all—love.

No matter how accurate the pattern of church life, how sound the doctrine, how manifest the gifts, or how aggressive the evangelism, apart from a true expression of the life of God in love, it is not what He wants in this world! Unless we somehow come back to this, we will miss the heart of all that God is and all that He desires to do.

Expressing true, self-denying, sacrificial love in our chaotic age is bound to be difficult. Add to all the other problems the necessity of gathering week after week in close intimate fellowship with people with whom you have little in common naturally, in an atmosphere where each is encouraged to open up and share—well, this certainly doesn't make it any easier. On top of this, the enemy will do all he can to destroy any expression of God's life. But all of this should have the effect of thrusting us more and more into total dependence upon the Christ who dwells within us. "Greater is He who is in you than he who is in the world" (1 John 4:4). He is the mystery of godliness and the hope of glory. We are just mirrors, reflecting the image of Christ. The source of that image must be His life. Faith is the key and Jesus is the "author and perfecter of faith" (Hebrews 12:2). More than ever before, we need to look to Him, to trust Him to be Himself in our lives and to expect Him to bring about on this earth the greatest expression of His life in His church that the world has ever seen!

19

WHAT NOW?

As I sit here writing this final short chapter, I wonder what your reactions are to what you have read. Perhaps, if some of these things are new to you, you are as surprised as I was when I was first introduced to them. Maybe you disagree, or you're just not sure yet. Or you might be one who has long seen and lived in these things and your heart is warmed and your convictions confirmed. I do feel confident that there will be some, however, who will read this book and wonder what to do about what they have read. It's for these that I am writing these closing words.

The first thing you should do is to take your questions to the Lord. Only those things in this book or any other which the Spirit makes real to your heart will be of any value in life. Have confidence that "the anointing which you received from Him abides in you, and. . .teaches you about all things" (1 John 2:27). God is able to show you His mind by the Spirit. My prayer is that He will quicken the truth to you and hide from your heart anything I may have interjected which is not according to His will for your life. Remember too that we all have backgrounds which tend to cloud our vision of spiritual things. Don't reject what I have shared only because it violates your background; take that to the Lord as well, asking Him to break through and show you any new truth He has for you.

I trust you realize that the heart of all I have tried to say is that we do contain His life. Begin to learn to live by that life, asking the Lord Jesus to help you discern between your own soulish human life and His divine life in daily living. Expect Him to be love in you where there has been bitterness, peace where there has been fear, joy where there has been sorrow.

Let Him be your power, your victory, your life in every situation every day. Learn to feed on Him, for He is the bread of life and the living water. His life in you is the new wine, the mystery of the ages, the explanation for the universe, and the only means of true godliness. Nothing is so important as to find and enjoy Jesus Christ as your life.

The next thing is to realize that God's desire for you is that you be a part of a group of believers who gather together to let Him be their life as a group. That new wine must have a new wineskin. If you don't have regular fellowship with a group of believers in an atmosphere where you can express with freedom what the Lord has given you in a true body-ministry, then begin to seek such a fellowship. If you will make it a definite matter of prayer, the Lord will lead you into something. There may already be some believers fellowshiping near you that you aren't even aware of. Or, as you pray, the Lord may begin to bring a few together to share along these lines. But don't panic if it doesn't happen right away. That which God wants must be born of the Spirit in travail, not just whipped together overnight by the organizational ability of some "leader." As you pray for the Lord to raise up an expression of His body in your area, you can be confident that you are praying according to His will and that He will answer.

To fit into such a fellowship and to communicate the things of God in this world you need to be clothed with the power of the Spirit and to receive gifts to equip you. Only you know your need here. Does the power of the Spirit rest upon you? If you have any doubt, remember that your heavenly Father wants to meet your need. You may also want to ask some other Christians to pray with you.

Many people ask, When I come into body-fellowship, should I drop out of the organized church? There is no one who can answer that question for you. I think the important thing is that you realize what the church really is and that you find a fellowship where Christ is truly head, where the desire of those involved is to share His life as an expression of His body in New Testament simplicity. You must have this, because it is central to the will of God for your life in many ways. If, when you have this fellowship, you can also stay in the organized church and be a sweet and loving testimony to the truths you have seen, this may be fine. But don't be there because you want to divide and destroy. If the Lord directs you to "missionary" activity in the organized church on the side, that's another matter. For many, however, this will not be the case.

When you do begin to fellowship in body-ministry, it won't be long before you find out that it is not the proverbial bowl of cherries. You see, God is building His church out of living stones, not of clay. Stones require a lot of chipping, grinding, and polishing before they become the kind of jewels that make up the wall of that holy city. Part of that polishing process is the rough and tumble of fellowshiping with one another. As I mentioned earlier, God uses the corporate life of the church to bring the cross to bear in the individual life. The purpose is to strike a deathblow at the expression of soulishness in you so that the life of Christ can be manifest. God uses the variety, the discipline of forbearing one another and submitting to one another, and even the soulishness of the other Christians to work out His purpose in your life. Whatever you do, don't run from it! I heard one fellow say recently that you start out with brothers, then they become friends, and finally enemies; then the Lord begins to work. I can't say it strongly enough: If trouble comes, don't run. Stay and let the Lord work it out. You may be right, but being right isn't enough. God has a work to do that goes beyond being right, and He will do that work right where you are. Anyway, people are all the same, so you'll just run into more of the same wherever you go. *Stay and let God build!*

These are exciting days. Christ is still building His church. He is coming again and when He comes it will be for a bride which has prepared herself. I believe with all my heart that ours may be the generation which will see a truer and greater expression of the body of Christ in this world than has been seen since the first century—new wine in new wineskins! I also believe there will be a great apostasy which will only heighten the contrast between that which lives by His life and that which has another life. Many feel that we are overdue for some real persecution in this country. Certainly our brothers and sisters are seeing it in almost every other country in the world. But whatever the ingredients for these last days, this one thing we know: God wants a people in this world who contain, live by, and express His own life. These people form His church, and the powers of death and the gates of hades shall not overpower them (Matthew 16:18).

> *"Hallelujah! For the Lord our God, the Almighty, reigns. Let us rejoice and be glad and give the glory to Him, for the marriage of the Lamb has come and His bride has made herself ready." And it was given her to clothe herself in fine linen, bright and clean; for the fine linen is the righteous acts of the saints. And he said to me, "Write, 'Blessed are those who are invited to the marriage supper of the Lamb'." And he said to me, "These are true words of God" (Revelation 19:6-9).*

NOTES

CHAPTER THREE

1. W. Ian Thomas, *The Mystery of Godliness,* p. 69.
2. Ibid., p. 72.
3. Norman Grubb, *God Unlimited,* p. 27.

CHAPTER FOUR

1. Watchman Nee, *The Normal Christian Life,* p. 127.

CHAPTER SIX

1. Dietrich Bonhoeffer, *The Cost of Discipleship,* p. 69.

CHAPTER SEVEN

1. Watchman Nee, *The Normal Christian Life,* p. 31.
2. Watchman Nee, *The Spiritual Man,* I:133.

CHAPTER ELEVEN

1. A. W. Tozer, *The Waning Authority of Christ in the Churches,*

CHAPTER TWELVE

1. W. J. Pethybridge, *A Lost Secret of the Early Church,*

CHAPTER THIRTEN

1. Alexander R. Hay, *New Testament Order for Church and Missionary,* p. 176.

CHAPTER FOURTEEN

1. Watchman Nee, *The Normal Christian Church Life,* p. 44.

CHAPTER FIFTEEN

1. Samuel Shoemaker, p. 184.

CHAPTER SIXTEEN

1. Watchman Nee, *The Normal Christian Church Life,* p. 98.
2. Ibid., pp. 97-98.

CHAPTER SEVENTEEN

1. Watchman Nee, *The Normal Christian Church Life,* p. 97.

APPENDIX

Because most of us have been so very far from the scriptural pattern of church life, the thought of returning to it often raises questions like the following.

WHAT IS THE PLACE OF WOMEN IN THE CHURCH?

The peculiar nature of the scriptural relationship of men and women is not just for the purpose of helping things to run smoothly, although it does have that effect. Remember that God created us to be expressions of Himself. Likewise, the church is to be an expression of Him, His life, and His nature. And in all aspects of our personal and church lives, God wants to use us to demonstrate something in the spiritual realm. This is very much the case with the matter of women in the church.

As I've stated several times, one of the biggest problems with the church is that Christ is often not really recognized as head. In Ephesians 5:23-24 Paul plainly states that Christ must be head and that the church must be subject to Him. He also states that Christ loves the church to the point of total self-sacrifice. But woven into this is the truth that the relationship between men and women is to be an earthly reflection of the heavenly relationship between Christ and the church (5:31-32). Christ is the head of the church. Man is the head of woman. Christ loves the church. Man is to love woman. The church is to be subject to Christ. The woman is to be subject to man. Now this is not a matter of anyone tyranizing anyone else, or of one being less important than the other. However, it is a matter of God having what He wants on this earth, and that makes it very important. So there is a difference in the role men and women are to play, and the difference is vital to God's ultimate plan for the human race. Just how does this difference work itself out in church life? There are three passages which show us:

Every man who has something on his head while praying or prophesying, disgraces his head. But every woman who has her head uncovered while praying or prophesying, disgraces her head (1 Co 11:4-5).

Let the women keep silent in the churches; for they are not permitted to speak, but let them subject themselves, just as the Law also says. And if they desire to learn anything, let them ask their own husbands at home; for it is improper for a woman to speak in church (1 Co 14:34-35).

Let a woman quitely receive instruction with entire submissiveness. But I do not allow a woman to teach or exercise authority over a man, but to remain quiet (1 Ti. 2:11-12).

The first thing we see from this is that women did pray and prophesy, and that this was not prayer in the closet or there would have been no need for special instructions as to her apparel. Prophecy is clearly a gift for the edification of the church (1 Co. 14:3-4) and Paul says, "You can all prophesy" (v. 31). On the day of Pentecost, Peter quoted Joel saying "Your sons and your daughters shall prophesy" (Ac. 2:37). And on that same day, the Holy Spirit caused the women as well as the men among the one hundred and twenty to speak with other tongues in a gathering of the church. Paul says that anyone who speaks with tongues in the church should also pray for the interpretation (1 Co. 14:13) so we can infer that women might also be used in that. So it is plain that there are at least three, perhaps four, things that women are permitted to do in fellowship with the church: pray, prophesy, speak with tongues, and interpret.

What then do we do with the second passage, which says to keep silent? Scripture doesn't contradict itself, so we must understand that this silence is not absolute, but refers to types of speaking. Obviously, Paul didn't intend them not to pray or prophesy or he wouldn't have bothered going special directions about it.

The key is found in the third passage, where Paul tells Timothy that he doesn't permit women to exercise authority over men. This ties in with the general principle that God wants to show something heavenly through this earthly relationship. If a woman exercises authority over a man, then the analogy suggests that the church can take charge over Christ.

The principle applies especially to two kinds of speech in the gatherings of the church. One is the matter of asking questions. If a man is teaching and a woman stops him to ask a question, she has already violated the principle in one way. But worse, she infers by her asking that her husband is not able to teach her what she needs to know at home, or that she is ahead of him spiritually, or that she is simply in rebellion and refuses to learn from him. No matter how it comes out, her husband is put down. On the other hand, if she simply waits to ask him at home, he can teach her privately if he knows the answer, or he can ask the question himself the next time the church gathers without upsetting the public demonstration of the heavenly analogy.

The other place this principle applies is where Paul forbids any woman to teach. Teaching is by its nature an authoritative ministry and the only way that women are permitted to exercise such a ministry is when the older women teach the younger to keep house (Titus 2:3-5). But to come to the church and say, "I am going to teach you what God has to say about. . ." is altogether out of the picture for women. It would be a complete reversal of all that God is saying through the church.

What can she do, then? As I see it, just about anything except ask questions or teach or anything else which would plainly show that her relationship to her husband was not according to the heavenly pattern. For instance, for a woman to bless and serve the Lord's Supper would be for her to take charge of the entire direction of the gathering. On the other hand, I don't think that a woman sharing a passage of Scripture that God has quickened to her an commenting on how it has helped her in her Christian life could be called teaching. God has a wonderfully wide range of ministries for the Spirit-filled woman in the church. If she understands what God wants to reveal through her relationship to her husband and if she walks in the Spirit, she will have no trouble staying within the proper bounds. Christ subjected Himself to the Father and was not humiliated but glorified. The church is expected to subject itself to Christ and it is not humiliated but built up. And the woman who seeks to please God, her husband, and the church will be honored by all of them.

WHAT ABOUT THE TRAINING OF THE CHILDREN?

We need to remember that the spiritual lessons we want our children to learn go much deeper than Bible stories or even doctrine. We want them to learn about and to receive God's life. If the Christian life were simply learning rules of ethical conduct, the catechism or Sunday school would be the best approach. But life is caught, not taught. Children have a great need to receive spiritual lessons from adults in whose lives they can see those lessons worked out in daily living. Otherwise they tend to develop the idea that spiritual truths have no relationship to living. We also need to be aware of the overwhelming tendency in our society to break down the family unit. Graded religious training can contribute to this tendency at the most vital point, worship and ministry.

One of the reasons that we have long used the specialist for training the children in spiritual things is that nobody was really convinced that the average parent could do it. So we put them in the hands of other parents. But parents who are involved in regular ministry to the body in the spiritual discipline of New Testament fellowship are parents who have something to give, who know how to minister life to others and to their children. Turning this over to someone else often has the effect of psychologically relieving the parents of responsibility and breaking down home worship and training.

We found that the children often get quite a bit out of body-fellowship and even participate from time to time. Recently, my nine-year-old daughter shared a meaningful experience she had had and it was a real contribution to the entire body. Also, children don't have to sit so still and be so quiet. They are free to sit on the floor if they like. They can leave the room to play elsewhere in the home for awhile, then come back later. Sometimes one of the parents slips out and spends some special time with the children, informally sharing with them something from the Lord. But this is spontaneous and never takes the place of the home as the training center.

One specific reference to the spiritual training of children in the New Testament is so clearly a picture of fatherly responsibility that Paul uses it as an illustration of his own fatherly ministry to the church. "We are exhorting and encouraging and imploring each one of you as a father would his own children, so that you may walk in a manner worthy of the God who calls you into His own kingdom and glory" (1 Th. 2:11-12). The Christians to whom Paul wrote were familiar with the figure of the father as the spiritual guide of the home. We have a great need to return to that today. "Fathers, do not provoke your children to anger; but bring them up in the discipline and instruction of the Lord" (Eph. 6:4).

WHAT ABOUT WEDDINGS?

There is no mention of weddings in either the Acts or the epistles, though Paul makes some important comments on marriage itself. We don't know how the early Christians actually held their weddings. We do know, of course, that it was entirely different from the usual wedding ceremony today, since there was no clergy class to "perform" the ceremony until many years later. Probably the Christians simply used the existing local customs. This seems to be what they did in many areas of life where the local customs did not conflict with the basic principles of God's purpose.

The Jewish marriage transaction at that time was a two-stage affair. The betrothal was primarily the legal aspect of the marriage. Documents were signed, the dowry given, and the marriage contract was legally binding from that time on, even though the couple didn't live together as man and wife until after the wedding, which came at least several months later. The wedding itself took the form of a feast at the groom's home. He and his friends brought the bride there from her parents' home, and after the feast they both gave testimony to their intentions to one another, after which they were led away to the bridal chamber as man and wife.

The current Christian custom of combining the legal and personal-religious aspects of marriage began to develop a few centuries later when the institutional church united with the state government to become the legal religion. Clergymen were recognized as officials of the state and their ministry in a wedding was both legally and religiously binding. Our society today still accepts this arrangement for the most part and thus clergymen are legally licensed by the state to perform wedding ceremonies which the state will recognize. In most states, the only alternative is a legal nonreligious "ceremony" performed by a justice of the peace or similar officer of the state.

Christians from church-in-the-home fellowships have tried to resolve this situation in various ways. Some have simply gone to the institutional church and had a clergyman marry them. Personally, I could not feel free to do that. Some groups have taken the step of registering the elders as clergymen with the state. There is a basic concept in both of these solutions which sounds like the world's system and which is alien to the church as God sees it. Also alien are many of the extravagant features of the modern wedding which have their foundation in pride and materialsim, and often cause unnecessary financial and emotional drain on the couple and their parents. I think there is need for a complete rethinking of the matter. Why not go to a justice of the peace to meet the legal requirements in a ceremony which would be the equivalent of the Jewish betrothal? Then, afterward, come together with the church for the real wedding—an exchange of testimony to one another and to God by the bride and groom, and the prayer, encouragement, and exhortations of the believers. Perhaps a charge to the groom by the bride's father and to the bride by the groom's father would be good. But the heart of the matter would be a commitment to one another and a commitment of their life together to God in the presence of the believers and in an atmosphere of the presence of Jesus, the Saviour, Lord, and head of their marriage and church. This would constitute the real and sacred consummation of their marriage. The earlier legal ceremony would simply be to satisfy the state and would remain in the same category with obtaining the license.

Marriage is a very holy thing, honored by God in every respect. But like everything in the Christian life, it is made holy by the appeal of sincere believing hearts and not be the sacramental blessing of any special person. Let believers follow the law of the Spirit of life in Christ Jesus, seeking

His guidance, and I am sure that God will direct them in the details of this important time of life.

WHAT ABOUT FUNERALS?

The thing that stands out in my mind concerning funerals is the totally nonchristian emphasis on the dead body which is so often the governing factor. This is understandable for people who live only in the present world and who have no hope, or only a vague hope of continuing life. But for the Christian, "to live is Christ, and to die is gain. . ., having the desire to depart and be with Christ, for that is very much better" (Phil. 1:21-23). Those who really believe this as a matter of life look not "at the things which are seen, but at the things which are not seen; for the things which are seen are temporal, but the things which are not seen are eternal" (2 Co. 4:18).

I fail to see why the body of a departed brother should enter into any observance of his memory among the believers. Call the necessary agents and request that they dispose of the body in an inexpensive, modest, and appropriate manner. Much of the usual expense incurred in funerals is due to feelings of guilt on the part of those remaining behind trying to make up for what they failed to do for the loved one while he lived. This condemnation has no part among believers. Whatever can be done for the departed one has already been done. Neither an elaborate ceremony or casket will do anything for him. Let's let the dead bury the dead.

Certainly we sorrow when a brother leaves us, because we will miss him. Yet we rejoice because he is in the arms of the Lord. So if desired, let the believers come together (without the corpse) and remember the brother with praise to God and a fresh commitment of their own remaining lives on earth to God. I know of one brother who departed and his family and friends came together for a "homegoing." Among other things, they sang the "Hallelujah Chorus," and though there were tears, there also was joy.

I've mentioned these questions because these issues are identified in the minds of many with the gatherings of the church. We have much light to discover yet in some of these areas and I don't mean these comments to sound arbitrary. We need to keep very close to the heart of the matter, and that is that all the Christian life and all the church life is intended by God to be the spontaneous expression of His own life in us.

BIBLIOGRAPHY

KEY

The purpose of this Key is to link the books in the Bibliography to the subject matter as it is covered in the *Quiet Revolution.* The underlined bibliography numbers indicate the key book on each subject.

CHAPTER	SUBJECT	BIBLIOGRAPHY REFERENCE
2	Creation of Man	2, 26, 30
3	Body, soul, spirit	2, 13, 23, 25, 26, 30
4	Christ in you	2, 13, 23, 30, 31
5	Dying to self	5, 13, 21, 23, 25
6	Water baptism	12
7	Blood—forgiveness	23
	Death of old man	2, 13, 23, 26
8	New birth	2, 13, 23, 26, 29
	Spirit "baptism"	3, 4, 12, 23
9	The life of faith	13, 23, 30
10	Believer's ministry	7, 10, 14, 19, 22, 27, 28
	Church history	1, 6, 14, 16, 28
11	Body of Christ	7, 14, 18, 27, 28
12	Church gatherings	3, 7, 10, 14, 18, 19, 22, 27, 28
	Ministry of women	18
13	Elders	10, 14, 22
14	Gifts of Spirit	7, 10, 14, 15
15	Evangelism	8, 9, 20, 27, 32
16	Finances	14, 21, 22, 29
17	Apostles	10, 22, 24
	Apostles' finance	22, 24, 29
18	Basis of fellowship	5, 7, 22
	Unity of the church	3, 7, 17, 22
	Church decisions	14, 18

BOOKS

An asterisk (*) indicates a book regarded as especially helpful for further study regarding New Testament Christianity today.

1. Allen, Roland, *Missionary Methods—St. Paul's or Ours?* Grand Rapids: Eerdmans, 1962.
2. Austin, Sparks, T., *What Is Man?* London: Witness & Testimony Pub., n.d.
3. Bartleman, Frank, *What Really Happened at Azuza Street?* Northride, Cal.: Voice Pubns., 1962.
4. Basham, Don, *Face Up with a Miracle,* Northridge, Cal: Voice Pubns., 1967.
5. Bonhoeffer, Dietrich, *The Cost of Discipleship,* New York: Macmillan, 1959.
6. Broadbent, E. H., *The Pilgrim Church,* Westwood, N. J.: Revell, n.d.

7. Carlson, Chester, *These My Brethren,* Northridge, Cal.: Voice Pubns., n.d.
8. Coleman, Robert E., *The Master Plan of Evangelism,* Westwood, N.J.: Revell, n.d.
9. Conant, J. E., *Every-Member Evangelism,* Westwood, N.J.: Revell, n.d.
10. Erickson, A. R., *New Testament Pattern and Practice,* Minneapolis: Bethany Fellowship, n.d.
11. Fromke, DeVern, *The Ultimate Intention,* Indianapolis: M.O.R.E., Inc., n.d.
*12. Frost, Robert, *Aglow with the Spirit,* Northridge, Cal.: Voice Pubns., 1965.
13. Grubb, Norman, *God Unlimited,* Fort Washington, Pa.: Christian Literature Crusade, 1962.
14. Hay, Alexander R., *New Testament Order for Church Missionary,* Audubon, N.J.: New Testament Missionary Union, 1947.
15. Horton, Harold, *The Gifts of the Spirit,* Springfield, Mo.: Gospel Pub. House, 1960.
16. Kennedy, John, *Torch of the Testimony,* Northridge, Cal.: Voice Pubns., 1965.
*17. Kurosaki, Kokichi, *One Body in Christ,* Northridge, Cal.: Voice Pubns., 1968.
18. Lang, G. H., *The Church of God,* London: Paternoster, 1959.
19. Lindell, John, *Thoughts on Christian Fellowship,* Northridge, Cal.: Voice Pubns., 1964.
20. Little, Paul E., *How to Give Away Your Faith,* Madison, Wis.: Inter-Varsity, 1966.
21. MacDonald, William, *True Discipleship,* Kansas City, Kan.: Walterick Pub., 1962.
*22. Nee, Watchman, *The Normal Christian Church Life,* Washington, D.C.: ISI Press, 1969.
*23. ---------, *The Normal Christian Life,* Fort Washington, Pa.: Christian Literature Crusade, 1957.
24. ---------, *The Normal Christian Worker,* Northridge, Cal.: Voice Pubns., 1965.
25. ---------, *The Release of the Spirit,* Indianapolis: Prem-Lit Co., 1965.
26. ---------, *The Spiritual Man,* Indianapolis: Christian Fellowship Pub., 1968.
27. ---------, *What Shall This Man Do?* Fort Washington, Pa.: Christian Literature Crusade, 1962.
28. Pethybridge, W. J., *A Lost Secret of the Early Church,* Minneapolis: Bethany Fellowship, n.d.
29. Pierson, Arthur T., *George Mueller of Britsol,* Westwood, N. J.: Revell, n.d.
30. Thomas, W. Ian, *The Mystery of Godliness,* Grand Rapids: Zondervan, 1964.
31. ---------, *The Saving Life of Christ,* Grand Rapids: Zondervan, 1961.
32. Trueblood, Elton, *The Company of the Committed,* New York: Harper & Row, 1961.